VICTORIAN
SUFFOLK

CLXX

VICTORIAN SUFFOLK

ALLAN JOBSON

ILLUSTRATED

ROBERT HALE · LONDON

Robert Hale & Company
63 Old Brompton Road
London, S.W.7

PRINTED IN GREAT BRITAIN
BY EBENEZER BAYLIS AND SON, LTD.
THE TRINITY PRESS, WORCESTER, AND LONDON

Love thy country, wish it well.
Not with too intense a care,
'Tis enough, that when it fell,
Thou its ruin didst not share.

George Bubb Dodington, Baron Melcombe
1691–1762

CONTENTS

ILLUSTRATIONS

9

FOREWORD

Victorian Suffolk crept in stealthily enough amidst peaceful seclusion. Few knew what was happening in the great outside world, or cared much about it. The reign started peacefully, slowly, at walking pace. It was to be a long reign, so that the fascinating little creature that took the throne on that June morning was to grow older and older—but never senile. When her Jubilee came about and all the pomp and circumstance surrounding it, those who were near enough to the steps of St Paul's, saw a little old lady with a bonnet drive up in a carriage for the Thanksgiving service.

Then came the end, unfortunately in war, and someone could write: "I shall never forget that bright winter morning when I looked out and saw the sad half-mast high flag on the tower, telling of the Queen's death—nor, later on indeed, the monotonous tolling from all the village steeples." Yet how much had happened between that span of years. It was a different England, as it was a different Suffolk.

Whether in the light of today's amenities one would like to have lived in those early years, is not at all certain. It was a spartan existence for the best of people, whether at home or travelling. (A good glimpse into those ways can be obtained from Augustus Hare's writings.) People must have been tough or they could not have survived. For example, medicine and surgery were in a deplorable state, and the country housewife, in her sagacious handling of remedies, must have been infinitely better off than her town sister. Whereas the doctor would have done his worst, she did her best, and pulled the patient through, but as for the poor, think of the life of a boy on a coasting vessel.

My father, born 1850, was a case in point. He was the
illegitimate son of a so-called surgeon (who died at 30), but his
grandfather was a surgeon of those days, and my father lived only
just round the corner from where they practised. As a very little
boy he was jumping off a heap of stones with other boys, when
he fell and dislocated his kneecap. What did they do? They took
him home, placed him on the table, hacked his knee about
without any anaesthetics, and lamed him for life. Presumably
they knew no better.

Then, of course, it was an age of great certainty, until Darwin
rather shattered its complacency. But it saw the rise of the Oxford
Movement, with the first of the 'Tracts of the Times' emanating
from the Deanery at Hadleigh under the inspiration of the
Reverend Hugh Rose. Then it was a great period for restoration
of country churches, far too drastic in treatment to be welcomed.
A notable example in Suffolk was that at Stradbroke, under the
guidance of the Reverend J. C. Ryle, afterwards Bishop of
Liverpool. However, perhaps it was as well they did something
about these old buildings because they were shockingly neglected.
And that went also for some of the halls, manors and farmhouses.

Some of the estates were vast, such for instance as that of
Arthur Maitland Wilson Esq., D.L., J.P. This is what was said
of him:

There are few gentlemen who are better known or more highly
respected amongst the country families of West Suffolk. He is Vice-
Chairman of the West Suffolk County Council, and the owner of
the charming and picturesquely situated demesne, Stowlangtoft
Hall, near Bury St. Edmunds. Mr Wilson is the eldest son of the
late Lt. Col. Fuller M. Wilson, of the 3rd. Battalion Suffolk Regiment, and is the sole owner of the Stowlangtoft estate, which in-
cludes the parishes of Stowlangtoft and Langham, and portions of
the parishes of Pakenham, Norton, Stanton, Badwell Ash, Bardwell,
Great Ashfield, Walsham-le-Willows and Hunston. The Hall is in
the Italian style, is situated in a beautifully undulating and well
wooded park, and it has the reputation of being one of the best
sporting estates in the County.

Add this: "Col. Nathaniel Barnadiston is a representative of the
family of Barnadiston or De Barnston, who were settled in the

Parish of Barnadiston before the Conquest, and at one time there were two Baronetcies in the family."

That Suffolk was in the war that clouded the last years of the old queen is evidenced by this: Major John Arnold Cuthbert Quilter, of the Grenadier Guards, son of Sir Cuthbert Quilter of Bawdsey Manor, served in South Africa during the Boer War, and distinguished himself at the Battle of Biddulphsberg, near Senekal, May 29th, 1900, when, after General Rundle's attack on the position, the Boers set fire to the Veldt. The incident was described in Divisional Orders as follows: "Lieutenant Quilter (2nd Battalion Grenadier Guards) and a party of men who volunteered belonging to the same regiment, rescued twelve wounded men, under heavy fire, from being burnt to death as they would otherwise have been by the grass fire."

This war was in many villagers' hearts, because the Suffolks were in it. I cannot refrain from quoting "Walberswick Notes" by Carol Christie on the subject, given by one of the local women characters.

" 'That there Bullard (Sir Redvers Buller), he'll get wowunded, I know he will. There! A wunnerful numerous people, them Bores! wunnerful numerous; they do say as how they shoot with bows and arrows!' She went on to comment on the names given to the children in consequence. 'A little baby belonging to one of her relations was to be called "Pretoria May", for Pretoria *may* be relieved in May'."

As a pointer to the social barrier of trade and profession, comes a description of the Right-Honourable Sir Saville B. Crossley, baronet, Privy Councillor, whose country seat was the Elizabethan mansion of Somerleyton Hall. Not once is it stated that he was a manufacturer of carpets.

One of the most interesting of these county celebrities was the Right-Honourable the Lord Gwydyr, whose seat was at Stoke Park, Ipswich. He was born in 1810, and at Queen Victoria's coronation was the official secretary to the Lord Great Chamberlain, a post he held until 1870. He retained all his faculties until an advanced age, could read without glasses and managed his estate himself.

When the Queen died the countryside presented a sorry spectacle. In 1874 the area under wheat had been in the region of

4 million acres, but by the time of her death had shrunk to less than half. No one who could get out of them stayed in the villages, and the towns thereby increased—although there was still a specialized population serving the needs of the country houses. It was generally estimated that the upkeep of a horse and a domestic servant cost about the same. In fact, as Sir Charles Petrie has pointed out, the countryside was dominated by the country houses—which had not yet become 'stately homes' for their owners lived in, and not off, them.

One of the most significant inventions, certainly from the point of view of the social historian, was that of the photograph. From these we are able to see what our forbears were really like, warts and all. The limners may have left us with a lot of portraits, but they probably had regard to the wrinkles. That is why the picture of James Woolnough (facing page 32) is so good. He kept the 'Angel' at Saxmundham—at least he didn't, it was his wife who kept it, while he looked after the cattle and stock. This is really a daguerreotype and I had the companion picture of his wife and child, but in endeavouring to clean it up wiped them off the plate. Woolnough, by the way, is a very old Suffolk name.

The sheet pasted on the back of his portrait reads as follows:

The celebrated American Photographic Studio, Patronised by the Leading Families in this part of England, now visiting this town for a fortnight only. The proprietor respectfully invites attention to his Portraits on Paper, Leather, Metallic Plates and Glass taken by the improved process, pursued by the great American Artists, and adopted by the Managers of the above establishment which insures a more perfect Picture with great dispatch, and freed from all imperfections in form and aberration in face.

Especial care will be bestowed in the colouring and finishing department, to give satisfaction and gain an extended patronage which has hitherto been accorded to the above.

Portraits for Brooches, Minatures for Lockets, Rings etc. Churches, Buildings, Paintings, Cattle etc copied Singly or Stereo-scopically.

Portraits taken at the residence of Parties if required without any addition to the economic prices charged at the Studio – lower than any Establishment of the kind travelling –

W. Stewardson, Printer, Little London Street, Norwich.

Just as the reign opened with great opportunities for the future, so it closed with even greater things to come. The Queen in her youth had welcomed those great advancements in science and technology, but she did not welcome the birth of that significant accomplishment, the internal combustion engine, that was to change the whole sphere of things. Her aversion to the motor car was very great, especially when she saw a photograph of her eldest son in an open motor wearing a top hat, which had been shaken or blown over his nose. She is reported to have said to the Master of the Horse, "I hope you will never allow any of those horrible machines to be used in my stables. I am told they smell exceedingly nasty, and are very shaky and disagreeable conveyances altogether." After all, one's vision goes so far and no further, one cannot see the end of the road.

> But the tender grace of a day that is dead
> Will never come back to me.

HARVEST CART IN SUFFOLK

Yow, Jack, bring them 'ere hosses here—
Get this 'ere waggin out;
I think the weather means to clear,
    So jist yow look about!
Come, put old Jolly to right quick—
    Now then, hook Di'mond on.
(There, chuck yow down that plaguy stick),
    An' goo an' call old John.
John bo', the Cart-shud close we'll try
    (Get yow upon the stack):
I'm sure the whate's by this time dry—
    Bring them 'ere forks here, Jack.
Blarm that 'ere chap! where is he now?
    Jest look yow here, my man,
If yow don't want to have a row,
    Be steady, if you can.
Ope that 'ere gate, Wish! Jolly-wo!
    Cop that 'ere rope up, Sam;
Now I'll get down an' pitch, bo', so
    Jump yow up where I am,
Load wide enough, mate—that's the style—
    Now, hold ye!—Di'mond!—wo-o!—
Jack!—that 'ere boy do me that rile—
    Just mind yow where you goo!
There goo a rabbit! Boxer, hi!—
    She's sure to get to ground.
Hold ye! Now then, bo', jist yow try
    To turn them nicely round.
Don't touch them shoves down! Blarm the boy!—
    You'll be in that 'ere haw!
That feller do me so annoy:
    But he don't care a straw.

How goo the time? I kind o' think!
    Our fourses should be here.
Chaps, don't yow fare to want some drink?
    There's Sue with the old beer!
The rain have cleared right slap away;
    An' if it hold out bright,
Let's work right hard, lads (what d'ye say?)
    An' clear this field to-night!

C. Laflin

I

THE COUNTY

The Royal Standard is flying from the Round Tower, for Queen Victoria is at Windsor.

Mary MacCarthy

The Victorian period, covering the longest reign in history commenced in a Georgian England and during the Long Peace, but the spirit of reform was growing and becoming very evident. The Parliamentary Reform Act of 1832 affected Suffolk, when the rotten boroughs of Orford, Aldeburgh and Dunwich were disfranchized. A new Poor Law came in in 1834, and in 1836 the General Registration Act allowed Dissenters civil marriages. In 1846 the failure of the potato crops in Ireland and the harvest in England forced Sir Robert Peel to introduce a bill for the repeal of the Corn Laws.

As my maternal grandfather was born in 1829 and died in October 1906, his life spanned the whole era. Moreover, he lived and died in the same village. As with all his associates, he was of pure Suffolk extraction, down to his very name, and a Victorian through and through. When he was born the privileges of life were in the hands of the few. However, as the reign proceeded conditions were more evenly distributed, though the aristocracy continued to govern—and did so to all intents and circumstances until the First World War changed everything.

In those very early days, when the Queen was a sparkling young woman, snipe abounded within a few hundred yards of Trafalgar Square. The route then, say from Saxmundham to London, for common folk, was by a hooded wagon and six horses. Tradition says the passengers wrote home from Melton the first night to tell their friends that so far the journey had prospered. The eastern part of Suffolk was little more than a sea of heath, and swedes and mangold were then unknown as agricultural produce.

One or two significant dates might be mentioned, although their effects on the rural life of Suffolk must have been long in tarrying. There was, for instance, the invention of the sewing machine by Elias Howe in 1841. The lucifer match came into use in 1835, but the greatest advance of all was the introduction of Roland Hill's Penny Post in 1840. The postage stamp was introduced at the same time, and, although it had adhesive on the back, it had to be cut out with scissors; perforation was not introduced until 1854. (A housemaid went home to spend her father's birthday. He was a gummer of postage stamps.) By 1897 a regular delivery was made to every house in the United Kingdom. Then, William Henry Fox Talbot invented the negative-positive process otherwise known as the calotype process, and the first photographs appeared in 1834 and '35. This discovery was to provide later historians with first-class documents of social history.

In 1841 the population of Suffolk was 315,073 and the number of houses were 76,499; uninhabited 3,931; building 301. By 1901 these figures had increased to 384,293 population and the inhabited houses to 83,778. Some of these so-called houses were the most awful hovels and can be traced even to this day in the form of sheds and outbuildings of a small farm or business premises. A few years ago there were people alive who could remember families or an old couple living in them. On the other hand, hundreds of the slightly better class still survive and have become by modernization the pride and joy of their owners. Loudon wrote: "A thatched cottage is an object of admiration with many persons who have not had much experience of country life." He went on to speak of the pests that invaded them, but the control of such things has been dealt with today.

Suffolk was essentially an agricultural county with a soil of such a varied nature—often variable in the same field—that it allowed the cultivation in some part or other of nearly every crop that would grow in the island. The county was celebrated for its wheat crops, whose success was said to be due to drainage and the peculiar system of drill husbandry. The usual method of drainage was to dig trenches and fill them with stubble, ling, straw and sometimes peat, which then supported the earth until it became compressed to form a firm arch. Even after the invention of tile drainage in the 1820s and 1830s the traditional Suffolk method continued to have its advocates, since it was cheaper and in some farmers' opinions equally durable. Sanfoin was also largely cultivated.

"As an agricultural county Suffolk can scarcely be surpassed." Thus wrote John Glyde in 1851. He went on to say: "Our stock has long been noted for its superiority and if this excellence is due to breed in the first instance, it must be acknowledged that no other influence than that of climate could have perpetuated it, for the same stock imported into less favourable regions is known to deteriorate rapidly."

In Raynbird's *Agriculture of Suffolk* (1849), the author says: "I can say this much for the Suffolk labourers that wherever I have been I have never seen their skill as ploughmen and drill workers surpassed and very seldom equalled; and it is merely the want of education that debars them from filling situations for which they are in other respects well qualified."

Considering the large number of labourers' wives that worked in the fields, it might be said that the most general employment for Suffolk females was agriculture, certainly around 1850. At certain seasons of the year they could be seen pulling turnips or beet, gathering stones, forking grass out of turnip land, dropping wheat, hoeing, planting peas and beans, making hay, gavelling, dressing corn, and even feeding stock.

Hours of work were generally from eight o'clock to four or six in the afternoon; ten hours in summer, eight in winter. Eight was the common time to begin, as it enabled the women to put their cottages in order in the morning and make arrangements for their being absent all day. The average wage was 7d. per day; during hay and corn harvest from 1s. to 1s. 6d. At Mildenhall, when employed dibbling, they could earn 1s. 6d. to 1s. 8d. It was the hardest work to do and lasted from three weeks to a month.

Employment of boys. At the age of 7 they went bird keeping and picking weeds off the land. A Mr Moore of Badley said: "Boys sometimes come at 2d. a day; little things that can hardly walk come with their fathers." One eyewitness said:

If you lived in the country as I do, you would sometimes see a sight which would make your blood run cold, and yet it is so common a sight that we country people grow accustomed to it. You would see a great lumbering tumbril, weighing a ton or two, with wheels nearly six feet high, loaded with manure, drawn by a great Suffolk cart horse as big as an elephant, and conducted by a tiny thing of a boy who can hardly reach the horse's nose to take hold of the rein, and if he can has neither strength nor weight to make such a huge monster feel, much less obey. Sometimes these little urchins are employed upon the high road, which is comparatively safe for them. It is when they come into the fields with deep wheel tracks, as deep nearly as half their little legs, it is turning into the gate spaces where the children are obliged to cling to the horse's bridle and stumble along tip-toe, that the danger is. One trembles to see the little wretches, knowing that if they should fall, or relax their feeble grasp of the rein, they must almost inevitably fall along in the cart rack, and the wheel would pass over them and jam [sic] them to a mummy. And why is all this peril incurred? Why are mere children of ten or eleven years old exposed to such perils? I hardly like to say why. Accidents nearly fatal have occured, but they do not seem to operate as a warning to those farmers who expose the lives of these poor children in order to pocket a few extra shillings weekly. We protect factory children amidst machinery. Are the lives of these clod-hopping boys less valuable.

This was from the *Suffolk Chronicle* for 3rd November 1855.

The 1851 census returned 5,092 farmers in Suffolk. There were not many large farms, although there were many large farmers, such as Mr Capon of Dennington, who held 5,000 acres of land. He had about 120 horses, and wages varied between 7s. 6d. and 10s. per week; horsemen received 1s. per week extra. Gleaning produced 4 to 8 bushels of wheat, and rent of cottages varied from £2 to £4 or £5 per annum. Some were merely hovels, made of clay, thatched, without ceilings or hard floors.

Here follows the income of a man and how it was spent. It was provided by a woman, whose family always appeared clean and neat, and whose children were brought up to industrious habits.

Robert Crick aged 42   9s. per week.

| Wife 40 | 9d. per week. |
| Boy 12 | 2s. per week. |

Boy 11	1s. per week.
Boy 8	1s. per week.
Girl 6	nil
Boy 4	nil
Total earnings	13s. 9d.

Expenditure: Bread 9s., potatoes 1s., rent 1s. 2d., tea 2d., sugar 3½d., soap 3d., blue ½d., thread etc. 2d., candles 3d., salt ½d., coal and wood 9d., butter 4½d., cheese 3d. Total 13s. 9d.

Although the Victorian period was the precursor of this present, particularly as regards scientific achievements and advancement, yet it was a horse-drawn age, and as such differs greatly from our own times. Moreover, Suffolk was distinguished from other counties in that it had a horse peculiar to itself, the famous sorrel, known as the Suffolk Punch; bred with the utmost jealousy because not every sorrel could be classed as a Suffolk horse.

The Earl of Stradbroke, writing in those early years, was one of the earliest breeders of high-class Suffolks in the county. He stated that a cart horse should "have a good head, neck well placed, shoulders lying back; should measure well round the girth; wide ribs, strong back ribs; a good wide back; tail well set on good wide hindquarters, long arms, short legs, good feet, attended to from the time of foaling. Colour, not a light chestnut; the red chestnut is popular, but a dark chestnut is generally the most hardy, and can accomplish most work."

And this is an old man's comment: "Yes, sir, they did say he was nice kind o' colt, but had na fa-et ye know sir. Oh yes, a verra pretty horse, but I like 'em with good fa-et. Don't you, sir?"

The *Suffolk Stud Book*, written about the '50s and published in 1880 by Herman Biddell, himself a farmer, gives us a very realistic picture of agricultural life in the early years of the reign, full of tradition, leisure and stability. It was a time of the aristocracy and the land, and a class distinction so pleasantly administered in the list of patrons of the volume. These range from marquis, earl, lord, baronet, knight, 'honourable', esquire to plain mister. For example the treasurer was an esquire, but the secretary was mister.

As the railways did not come in until the '40s, certain hostelries, such as Kesgrave 'Bell', would be described as a baiting house between Ipswich and Woodbridge on the Yarmouth turnpike. A travelling horse's route would be from country inn to country inn, such as, say, from Kirton 'Greyhound' to Martlesham 'Lion', the 'Queen's Head' at Woodbridge, Saxmundham 'Bell' and the Crown Inn, Framlingham.

This of a farmer: "He was chiefly celebrated for driving his four stallions in a team together, and tradition draws a picture of the four standing by the alehouse door, each with a foreleg strapped up while the teamster himself stepped in to see who was in the room with the sanded floor."

The great foal show at Woolpit Fair was the most noted of the year but was falling in reputation by the seventies. This formed the subject of one of E. R. Smythe's major pictures.

An American who came over here to buy horses was so impressed with what he saw when he reached the eastern counties that he remarked: "No wonder you are such capital farmers. You are brought up to farming; your fathers were farmers; you make your sons farmers—you have been farming for generations."

Farming in those early years of the reign was a tremendous business, for it must be realized they were agriculturists in the palmy days of unmolested prosperity. Wheat was at £4 a coomb, and wool 3s. a pound, prices with which they were satisfied. One of them described it as, "about betwixt the bark and the tree—fair living prices as we thought them then".

And, of course, the farmers lived well, although their poor labourers who exercised such a skill and affection for the work did not. For instance, a farmer in his younger days did not think himself anyways singular if he took two bottles of port after a two o'clock dinner. In fact he was considered a singularly temperate man. No wonder their nags took them home, unaided by guiding reins since they knew the way, while the farmers slept.

One of the famous farmers of the *Stud Book* was a Thomas Crisp, who farmed at Gedgrave, Butley Abbey and Chillesford Lodge. His success ran from "full aged horses to the best six cut geraniums". The writer, needless to say, a farmer himself, described the set-up:

At Butley, nineteen cart foals were in one meadow, all bred on the premises. In an adjoining yard were another nineteen full-aged white boars. But the place to spend a couple of hours was among the horses at the Hill Farm, Chillesford. I have seen eleven stallions led out one after the other.

The marvellous stories of his shipments for abroad were amptly testified by the porters at the railway station. One day every horse box within call would be telegraphed for to Wickham Market, for a consignment of Suffolk horses to one of the colonies: the next week a whole menagerie of animals would be sent off to Prussia. Again, a visitor to Butley would be startled by the sight of a row of wheat stacks at some off-hand occupation,[1] the growth of a year long since forgotten by any miller in the County; and strange tales were told of incredible clips of wool which had seen every shade of variation, from 10d. to 2s. 6d. a pound. Curious grasses of rapid growth and enormous yield would be raised from seed. Another season when flockmasters were starving under sunny skies and dew-less nights, strange tales would go from market to market, telling how the poorest, dryest and most wretched walks on the Tangham farm were knee deep in sheep feed, a luxurious herbage, the very name of which not one in ten had ever heard.

Crisp died in the hunting field in 1869.

When Crisp lived at Chillesford Lodge all the farms in that quarter were game farms. This term was used to express a state of things scarcely to be credited. It was in the time of the Marquis of Hertford, who owned the land and Sudbourne Hall. Stover stacks close to the premises were undermined by the hares till they had to be hurdled round to save the remnant from burying the swarms that would come for a meal on a frosty night. Not a turnip could be left unclamped after October, and boys had to keep the pheasants from the pea sticks. There were hares there at that time grey with age, with teeth turned up outside the jaw like the tusks of a wild boar. In 1849 3,000 were killed on the estate between Monday morning and Saturday night, and on one occasion 240 were killed in three hours, and then forty more, alive and hungry, were counted on a field close by where the slaughter had just taken place. They were coursed with grey-hounds till at last the dogs would wag their tails, turn their heads and refuse to run another hare.

* i.e. in out-of-the-way places.

Crisp sent a wonderful sow to the International Show at Paris in 1855, good all round from nose to rump's end and enormously fat. The judges all agreed there was nothing to compare with her, but withheld the prize as being "too fat to breed". On the way home she gave birth to a litter of eleven pigs before she reached Dover, and what was more brought them all up. They made nearly enough money to buy a small farm.

Another remarkable man of the time was Kersey Cooper, agent for the Duke of Grafton; a man who could farm 1,300 acres for himself and as many again for his landlord. "He did not farm on foot, and when on horseback he did ride a foot pace." He always attended one market in a week and sometimes two; he could manage an estate of 14,000 acres and see to every detail at the mansion as well; and was dearly fond of a day with the Suffolk hounds. Fox hunting was almost the one source of recreation he allowed himself. But he was dead at 54, having pushed himself too hard.

The weather seemed different in those days, with scorched up summers and terribly hard winters. In the hot months feed for the animals would be a great problem, and had to be sought. Kersey Cooper used to tell what today is an immortal story against himself, so compact of the true Suffolk character, when grooms and stock men were individualists. One of these was old Boon, the Butley shepherd.

It was such an exodus that Kersey Cooper met hard by the scene of one of Bloomfield's tales, when

"The lawns in Euston Park were dry,"

the dust ankle deep, and not a blade of grass to be found. One sultry evening in the latter part of July, Mr Cooper was out for a drive. "First I met a drove of colts—thirty, forty, fifty, I should think—more than I could count. Then came a hundred beasts—cows, lean bullocks, young things; foot sore, tired, and hungry as they could be; followed by the biggest flock of sheep I ever met in a road in my life. They were like the flocks of Abraham. At last came old Boon, leading a pony and cart with half-a-dozen skins and two lame sheep."

Boon was a tall man—6 feet 1 inch—and stooped a good deal, or rather leaned forward and plunged along in a slop down to his shoes like a man with sore feet on flint stones, and always walked with his eyes on his boots.

"Well my good man, and whose, in the name of goodness, are all these things you've got here?"

Boon pulled up, took his eyes off the ground, and said very slowly—"Well they belong to my marstar."

"But who is your master?"

"My marstar sar? Why, the gentleman that own all these couts and ship and things!"

"Well, where are you going with these ship and things?"

"I'm going arter some feed my marstar ha' bowt for 'em."

"And where are you going tonight—you can't lie on the road, can you?"

"Oh dear, no sar—there's too many on 'em to lay i' the rud—I can't lodge 'em i' the rud."

"Well, well, shepherd, as long as they are not going to mine I don't know that I've any business with it—good night."

"Good night sar—but I was just a going to say *pra-ay could you tell me where a mistar Karsay Cooper live some where in these parts.* I was to go to him for a night's lodging?"

The most abject apology, and profuse were the explanations that he "ha'nt the la-est idea who I was a speaking tu, but you know sar, my marstar al'ays tell me not to know nothing when anybody ax me about my business. He said he thowt you had a *little midder close to the house* that 'ud du nicely." And in the "little middar" the mixed multitude lodged, and little was left but the soil when they passed on the next day for another stage.

But the feeding from home in these unmanageable numbers is an anxious business, and the brazen skies and parched fields of 1868 told their tale on the sheep that had to be brought to the hammer at the Butley sale the following year.

Do you think they realized they were living in a great age? Yet time was passing, slowly, oh so slowly; and perchance the old men lamented the years of yesterday when things were done differently. Even so, they had developed from primitive practices; methods had not always been the same. The days of grandfather loomed largely in the past. The machine was creeping like a caterpillar into the scheme, and, like a caterpillar, was but the chrysalis that was to emerge as the butterfly in golden harvests and crowded stackyards, on which the harvest moon never shone more brightly or softly. For one thing, they rid themselves of the incubus of the parson with his tremendous power of entry into the harvest fields and his claim for the tenth shoof and the tenth piglet. In one matter they differed from their ancestors, in that they are limned for all time by means of the daguerreotype and later the calotype portrait of themselves in their characteristic clothes, with their sharp eyes, shrewd old faces and silent tongues.

> So have I heard the cuckoo's parting cry,
>   From the wet field, through the vext garden-trees,
>   Come with the volleying rain and tossing breeze:
> "The bloom is gone, and with the bloom go I."

The census of 1851 was more complete than those before, and was the first to give details such as places of birth. As far as Suffolk went it included three people in Eastern Bavents, and the eight inhabitants of Havergate Island. The increase in population was 21,855, but the county was not so prosperous as in 1841. The number of uninhabitated houses had increased by 755. It was stated that many of these tenements were in so dilapidated a condition as to render them unfit for habitation. The greater conveniences of many of the modern houses induced numbers of the people to desert the old tenements in which their forefathers had long resided.

Bachelors formed 25 per cent of the male population. Glyde says: "A few of our people are born, live and die in the same dwelling, many in the same parish, and the majority in the same county." Yet migration was taking place, because, although 337,215 persons were enumerated in the county, 384,446 persons in England and Wales belonged to Suffolk by birth. It was evident that Suffolk sent large numbers of her population to other counties, which indicated want of employment. There were 32,229 in London alone.

The list of employments is of great interest. In the literary class there were only 2 authors, but 22 editors. Artists numbered 23 above 20 years, 7 below. Of domestic servants there were 260 female tailors, 294 female shoemakers and 110 female glovers. Railway traffic accounted for 222 men—evidence of its infancy. There were 15 cork cutters, 461 sawyers (top and bottom), 229 coopers, 131 basket makers, 450 thatchers, 147 rope makers, 1,064 millers, 540 maltsters (who would have worn the red stocking caps) and 241 brewers. Agriculture embraced 51,564, to include 1,365 indoor servants and 413 shepherds. In the seven years 1839–45 the men who signed the registers with marks numbered 46 per cent, women 52 per cent.

Glyde had this to say about neighbourliness:

> The actual services of the poor to one another, among females especially, is truly admirable; the trouble they take, the anxiety they endure, and the sacrifices they make, are unparalleled among the middle classes. The tradesman's wife relieves poverty by a pecuniary donation; the labourer's wife gives personal aid. They often nurse their neighbours in sickness without fee or reward, and help to feed the children out of their scanty means. Suffering and privation, though it breeds harshness towards their superiors, strengthens their sympathies towards their neighbours, and those best acquainted with the working classes in villages agree that the sympathy of the poor is the best alleviation of the sufferings of the poor.

After the extraordinary hot summer of 1846, the deaths in the last quarter were numerous, 29 per cent above the mortality of the corresponding quarter of 1845. October was wet, November mild until the 7th. Epidemics of typhus and influenza set in, bronchitis prevailed, and the potato disease re-appeared.

During 1840–42, 1848–9, 153 died of smallpox, 330 of measles, 1,097 of scarlatina, 510 of whooping cough, 490 of diarrhoea, 129 of cholera, 1,692 of typhus, 292 of influenza. Typhus was a regular visitor, generally causing between 300 and 400 deaths annually. The deaths from consumption in Suffolk females was far above the average of England. However, Suffolk could boast exemption from the ague which prevailed on the Essex coast, mainly arising from the gravelly and chalky bottom that existed along the coast. The report ends up with the astounding statement that "it must be recorded that the compulsory Vaccination Act is a failure".

Infant mortality was the common fate of large families, and did not reach its height until 1899. It might also be recorded that the last cases of plague in England broke out in north-east Suffolk: in 1906 at Chantry Farm Cottages and Brickhill Terrace Cottages, Shotley; Lower Street Trimley in 1909–10; Turkey

Farm, Freston, 1910; Naval Barracks, Shotley in 1911; and Warren Lane Cottages, Erwarton in 1918.

The heartless crime of arson (destroying crops) was the principal offence in malicious offences against property, and to some extent was peculiar to Suffolk. In the five years ending 1842 there were six cases. These rose in the next five years ending 1847 to eighty-three, and by 1852 had fallen to sixty-one. The year 1844 was one of intense alarm to owners and occupiers of farms. Fires were of almost nightly occasion during the long evenings. The occupiers of land lived in a state of nervous excitement, looking about their premises every night before retiring to rest, apprehensive of the crops being destroyed. The corn stacks were placed in fields, a distance from each other, and away from buildings, so that if one should be fired the others might escape. In several instances the property set on fire belonged to agriculturists who had thrashing machines on the premises. During the year 1844 the crime of incendiarism prevailed extensively, almost throughout Suffolk.

It was stated that pauperism and crime in Suffolk were above the average in the kingdom. The Duke of Grafton stated in evidence before the Parliamentary Committee on the Game Laws that it was a proverb in Suffolk that "Poaching is the root of all evil". In 1851 a man was liberated from Bury jail after his twenty-first imprisonment for poaching; he boasted he had eaten eighteen Christmas dinners in prison. Another, only 20 years of age, had been fourteen times in prison, chiefly for poaching.

The villages of Snape and Sudbourne afforded particular instances. Smuggling had been a favourite occupation of a large number of labourers in the district, and the great quantity of game kept up by gentlemen of the neighbourhood, induced others to become practical poachers. These influences, combined with the scale allowance, had caused a number of resolute and daring paupers to reside in the village. Chaplains and governors confirmed the opinion that the Game Laws had made more criminals than any other system.

Some of the cases of larceny were of the most petty description: a married and also a single woman for stealing meat, a mother and daughter for egg stealing; a widow for stealing a faggot of wood, another widow for stealing nineteen turnips. But there was no true bill against a widow for stealing a gimlet, and a poor old dame 75 years of age for larceny of the value of 2d. A child only 11 years of age, who lived at Woodbridge with his stepmother, was committed for trial for obtaining one bushel of coal under false pretences. In 1841 the percentage of larcenies was greater in Suffolk than in any other county in England.

But, Glyde asks, "what is the reason that the law knows so much of the thieving propensities among the children of the lower classes, and scarcely any instance in the upper classes? The one is brought before a parent or instructor, the other before a magistrate."

Colonel Bence said: "My opinion is that want of employment has done more to demoralize the labouring part of the community, especially the younger part of it, than anything else. Where work is found them—where they are well looked after, fair wages paid, and an interest felt in their welfare—there you will find very little crime." These were wise and timely words, because it was noted that the Earl of Stradbroke, Sir Fitzroy Kelly, M.P., the Reverend E. R. Benyon and others, erected cottages for labourers on their estates, with due regard to the comfort and convenience of the poor.

This brings to mind that the Constabulary for the Eastern Division of Suffolk was established in 1840, with seventy-two constables, located in fifty-two districts, the headquarters being at Saxmundham. For West Suffolk it did not come into being until 1845, with eight sergeants and sixty constables and with headquarters at Bury. There was only one policeman at Sudbury; he received a salary of 18s. a week. He was notified in 1854 that he was no longer needed, and the gaoler took his place.

The extent of the Poor Law system was such that during the eight weeks of January and February 1853, there were 1,419 able-bodied men relieved in the Agricultural Union of Hoxne, an average of 177 weekly. In one week alone the number was as high as 294. This step of the farmers putting off the men naturally aroused the evil passions of the labourers, and so strong was the feeling excited, that, in cases of incendiary fires, they were the last persons that would aid in extinguishing the flames. Sympathy towards employers could not be expected from men when it was known that during the slack season many would be cast on the parish for their means of support.

In Cosford House of Industry the women on washing days were each allowed 5 pints of strong beer, in addition to the usual allowance. (How their old tongues must have clacked.) At Bulcamp ten milch cows were kept, and the paupers were supplied with milk and butter of the finest quality. There was also a regular licensed shop for the sale of tea, tobacco and snuff, kept by the female pauper. This had been permitted for years. The stock was regularly filled up, and the shop was inside the house. It was only natural that the remark crops up: "We have a large class of permanent and hereditary paupers."

There was a marked difference between the cottages in the 'open' and those in the 'closed' villages. On estates such as the Duke of Grafton's, the Marquis of Bristol's and Lord Cadogan's— as we have seen in the estates of the Earl of Stradbroke, Sir Fitzroy Kelly and the Reverend E. R. Benyon—the cottages were well built, kept in excellent repair, and provided with good gardens, sheds (what would a countryman have done without a shed?), outhouses, closets and wells, and often let for £2 10s. or £3 10s.

In the open villages it was otherwise, and one had to take pot luck. Even so, a great deal depended on the woman of the house; some would make a palace out of a pig-sty, others a pig-sty out of a palace. At a public meeting at Barrow a labourer gave the following particulars of his house: "I have to shift my bedstead to stop the rain. My room is 7ft. 6ins. by 6ft. 9ins. There are two bedrooms both this size. Twenty-one people go to one closet."

Agricultural associations began to appear as early as 1831, when the East Suffolk Association was formed. West Suffolk followed two years later, and the two amalgamated in 1856 into the Suffolk Agricultural Association. Their objects were the "Aid and Advancement of Agriculture, the Incitement of Skill, Industry and Good Conduct among Cottagers, Servants and Labourers in Husbandry, and the Incitement of Enterprise and Emulation among the Owners and Occupiers of Land."

Premiums offered by the East Suffolk Association for 1849 included in Class VI: "Mr. Richard Garrett, of Leiston, offers a premium of £3 to the man who manages and keeps in the best

James Woolnough, landlord of the Angel Inn, Saxmundham in 1861

A Victorian plough team. Note the fly nets across the horses' backs

Bill, dated 1860, from Richard Garrett and Son, Leiston Works near
Saxmundham

working order, his employer's drilling, horse hoeing, chaff-cutting, thrashing, grinding and general agricultural machinery."

Class VII was for shepherds. "To the shepherd who shall have reared from not less than 400 park-fed ewes put to the tup, the greatest number of lambs, with the smallest loss of ewes, up to the first of June, 1849. £2."

This brings us to the agricultural machinery invented and produced by R. Garrett and Son, of Leiston Works, who won the principal prize of £50 for the best portable steam engine, for thrashing and other agricultural purposes. Together with the prize of £25 for the best thrashing machine at the Royal Agricultural meeting at Norwich, in July 1849. The firm also gained prizes for the best corn drill, turnip drill, the best drop drill, for depositing seed and manure and the best horsehoe on the flat.

Incidentally, this is what was said in the *Stud Book*:

Mr. Richard Garrett of Carleton Hall, is one of the most spirited supporters of Suffolk horses now in the field. His winnings in the show-yard for the last few years have exceeded those of any of his brother exhibitors. The name is an old sound in the agricultural world; from South America to the shores of the Black Sea; from the far West of the United States to the corn growing districts of British India; in the most Northern provinces of Russia where cereals form an item in the products of Agriculture; in Australia; in Egypt—wherever wheat is grown, and there is capital enough to purchase a portable engine to thrash it, there the firm of Garrett and Sons is a familiar name. And not only is it in out of the way spots in distant hemispheres, but in every county in England where science goes hand in hand with practice—wherever the drill or horse-hoe is used there the name of the "Leiston Works" is a household word. So far as the outside world is acquainted with the firm of Messrs Garrett it is in connection with this branch of industry, and those who knew it only in years gone by associate the headship of the establishment with that shrewd-headed, far-seeing man, who having made the name known all over the civilised world took his place in his own country among the class which everywhere beyond its borders is the envy of all—the English country gentleman.

Mr. Garrett farms largely. Scotts Hall, Westleton, the Brook Farm, Saxmundham and Carleton Hall Park make a fine occupation. There is plenty of room for the young stock, and plenty to do for the old ones. Nearly twenty years ago Mr. Garrett's name appeared in the sale catalogues as the purchaser of choice lots of Suffolks, since which he has gradually been improving his stud and adding something from all the best stables as opportunities offered. It was not till 1869 that he went boldly to the front as a breeder and bought the best horse of the day to keep him from going out of the country. That year he purchased Crisp's Cup Bearer at the July sale at Butley Abbey. . . . When prize after prize fell to Cup-bearer in Mr. Garrett's hands no one's victories were hailed with more hearty congratulations than his. But such brittle wares as stud horses, which year after year go the rounds of showyards, do not last for ever.

Richard Garrett was obviously one of Suffolk's characters, wearing distinctive large hats at these agricultural shows. (They are, or were, to be seen at Leiston municipal offices.) His brother Newson of Snape and Aldeburgh fame was another, who fell out with Richard, as he did with everyone else in turn. The two had married sisters, who kept the peace between them, Newson's wife being a real 'old dear'.

James Smyth of Peasenhall began as a wheelwright repairing Suffolk drills. With his brother Jonathan of Sweffling they perfected a new type, with coulters which, instead of being fixed, could be raised and lowered for different widths of work. They sent travellers about the country to demonstrate the drill and undertook contract work for 2s. 6d. an acre.

Two farms in Suffolk figured in the Royal Commission of enquiry in 1828 and 1836. The first belonged to J. G. Cooper of Blythburgh. Arthur Young described this farm—Westwood Lodge—as without exception the finest farm in the county; it amounted to 1,600 acres. The second was at Ingham on the western side. In 1820 this was between eleven and twelve hundred acres.

The deplorable conditions under which some of the Suffolk labourers lived and worked accounted for the way in which they rallied to the standard of Joseph Arch. He was born in 1826 in Warwickshire, an agricultural labourer, who became a prize-winning hedge-cutter and a Primitive Methodist local preacher. The first Agricultural Labourers' Union was established at Leamington in 1872. Suffolk unions soon sprang up, and were so well established that Essex and Suffolk farmers formed a Farmers'

Defence Association. Skirmishes between employers and employed began in 1873, which were to culminate in the Agricultural Lock-out of 1874. At Woodbridge, all the labourers on strike, many accompanied by their wives and sons, all wearing blue rosettes, met on the Market Hill.

It was written at the time that everything on the hill and its neighbourhood, for the time being, was union—union gingerbread, union rock; and Fanny Frost sold union shrimps. Each vendor of these commodities wore 'the blue', thus securing a lucrative trade, and every ferryman plying between Sutton and Woodbridge, did a big stroke of business. The landlord of the 'Cock and Pye', drew many a barrel so dry that its insides were stark naked.

A letter from the Bishop of Manchester condemning the action of the farmers, was published in *The Times* on 2nd April 1874. This brought a spirited reply from Lady Stradbroke on behalf of the farmers, alleging that the labourers had no cause for complaint. Indeed, she painted an idyllic picture and told the bishop to mind his own business. Naturally she was supported by certain farmers, although one had the courage to support the men—viz. Mr Purcell FitzGerald, whose opinion was shared by his brother Edward, the translator of the *Rubaiyat*.

One great peaceful and constructive voice came out of the commotion, and that from one of Suffolk's large landowners— Sir Edward Kerrison. He commenced his letter to *The Times* with: "In a desert of strikes and lockouts my property forms a sort of oasis", and proceeded:

Men should be paid by the hour or by piece work, with the exception of special harvest arrangements, when higher wages are always paid. . . .

The whole labour question as now existing must be divested of all those benevolent and charitable adjuncts which with the most praiseworthy but most mistaken views are imported into it; they only divert the real question at issue, that of wages, which of necessity must henceforth be based upon commercial principles.

I have the authority of the farmers on my property to say that the working men employed by them, whether members of Unions or not, have throughout these trying times conducted themselves in a most satisfactory manner.

These proposals were supported by the Bishop of Manchester in a second letter, dated 20th April 1874.

As a result of this agricultural war—actually whilst it was in progress—Lord Stradbroke convened a meeting for 21st April 1874 at Ipswich, to create a Suffolk Provident Society to replace the many village societies. This was finally founded and registered in April 1875, Lord Waveney being the first president.

In the middle of the century, the labouring poor of the county were comparatively uninstructed. In 1851 143 parishes were described as being in a state of educational destitution. In numbers of parishes the schools were entirely supported by the incumbents; in others the farmers would not subscribe a penny towards their maintenance, and many of the gentry were tardy of their support. Out of 300 persons married in Hartismere in 1848, 175 signed the register with marks.

There was a certain amount of absenteeism in Suffolk. For instance, the Marquis of Hertford owned land in Sudbourne and Orford, but had not lived in the hall for many years. Although he received a large rental, no school was established by his efforts or advice. The Earl of Ashburnham was the owner of several thousand acres around Needham Market. He visited the district in 1853 after an absence of eleven years. The school received some aid from him but not comparable to his receipts. At Bramford, Sir Philip Broke was the owner of nearly 2,000 acres, but did little towards the education of the poor of that parish, where the schoolmaster received £20 a year, partly paid by the children's pence.

The parish of Framsden was another, where John Tollemache, M.P., owned 1,300 acres and in addition had the rectoral tithes of £500 per annum. Yet, with a population of 800 persons, there was no school until 1852. Nacton had a population of 901 and nearly 1,100 acres were owned by George Tomline, but there was no school there in 1851.

Sunday schools shine out rather distinctly in the darkness. In March 1851 there were no less than 541 Sunday schools, with 37,470 scholars, and 3,695 teachers. One of the most remarkable features was the number of teachers engaged in this voluntary work, giving up scanty leisure to devoted services.

There were also a few evening schools, classes at mechanics' institutes and mutual improvement societies. None had free admission, and the charges varied from less than 2d. a week to 5d. and upwards. A Suffolk Village Reading Room Association was established with headquarters at Ipswich. Needham Market, Clare, Leiston and Yoxford, had each an institute and reading room. At Yoxford essays were read and discussed for the purpose of stimulating the members in the acquisition of knowledge.

The coming of the railways was the great divide between the old and the new—in fact they changed the face of England. My grandfather could have seen and heard of the railroad, as it was then called, creeping up from Ipswich. When conditions in agriculture worsened, it was those railways that took villagers to the towns that were growing at the expense of the villages. My grandfather would hardly have thought when he walked over to see those navvies at work with pick and shovel, that it was by that means his daughters would all leave the nest and make their way to London, my mother being the pioneer. She had loved her old home, with its sweet-smelling fields, its old-fashioned way of life and its lovely food. But, truth to tell, she never wanted to return, save to see again her own people, gather the wild flowers that she loved, talk the old language and eat a few Suffolk rusks, spread with a nob of Suffolk butter. Then, as has been the case with every generation, the talk would be of the glories of yesterday, interspersed with laughs and tears. To her it had been mignonette all the way, as L. E. Jones put it.

The old language and habits persisted until Edward VII succeeded his mother. When the sky looked stormy they used to say, "Thass whully dark oover Will's mother's." Of a drought, "Thet hood [hold] dry, Jim" "Thet thet du, Tom bor". [Meaning that it does.] But "Yow'll write an' let us know how ye git on together."

Or of an icy cold winter with such a frost as the oldest could never remember. "Coold, masters, whoi thet should be stammin cold! Look yew hare tergether; the ould sun ha' tunned tew far tew the north, he hev!"

And this for sheer classicism: "Wh' lor', bor, yow fare t'bee s'trange. Wh' darn ya' ole skull, I now yow werry well. My fa' he now ya' fa' he kep a dickey. Hee one da' hult a stoon agin a guce, an' he kilt 'er ded, an' my fa', he sez, sez hee, thet he worn't

t' kum ower hisn troschel agin. An' n' moor he didn't." Which
being translated means: "Why, lor, boy, you seem to be strange.
Why darn your old head, I know you very well. My father he
knew your father. Your father kept a donkey. He one day threw
a stone at a goose, and killed it, and my father said he wasn't to
cross his threshold again. And he didn't."

Then there is the story of the old man who had his eye
examined. " 'I aren't agoin' fur tew hut yew, Butters, bor,' he
say, an' he tuk a grut owd light as wur set on his hid, an' thet
shin'd inter moi eyes a rum un; thet thet did, fit tew blind un.
But lawk! iver sin thet dai I ha' had the wind in moi hid; an' I
shall niver be no bitter this side o' the grave.' "

And there was the account of the Unionists who left for a better
world: "When they got to London, Woodbridge worn't nothin'
tu it, an' as fer Allerton [Alderton], whoi it might jist as well shet
up altogether." But the writer "Din't in the leastest doubt that
there wur as nice fook there as anywhere else, ony tha wornt
bred to't."

John Cordy Jeaffreson, 1831–1901, drew a most delightful
picture of East Suffolk before the coming of the railways; and,
according to him, the extinction of the small landowners blighted
the life of our small provincial towns and robbed them in the same
generation of their old-world sociability.

He described himself as having been born at Framlingham in
the woodlands of Suffolk. This, of course, refers to the magnificence of the many fine oaks that grew in this district, which
were particularly noticeable in shipbuilding times, when the
wooden walls of England were so important. He says: "In my
boyhood (say 17), I drove a carriage-and-pair through the hollow
stem of an oak in the parish of Cretingham." From the *History of
Framlingham* he quotes: "The Market Hill is nearly an equilateral
triangle and very spacious, on each side of which are several
genteel residences with many respectable shops; the side fronting
to the south stands upon a terrace or causeway, and is skirted with
a row of lime trees."

He points out the prosperity that came to shops even in country
villages, resulting in the creation of family fortunes. He instances
the Kilderbees of Framlingham with their shop on the Causeway,
and that of a John Cordy with another at Worlingworth, a purely

agricultural village. "He sold tea and Suffolk Bang (the poorest and hardest kind of cheese) by weight, poplins and bombazines by long measure." He had started as a weaver. Moreover, the leading draper in a small market town would also act as a banker and bill discounter.

The shop in those days was a general shop, in which people could buy groceries, drapery, cheese, butter, eggs, candles, tobacco, snuff, beaver hats, felt caps, umbrellas, gloves of all sorts, hair powder, hosiery. Behind would be an office for banking services.

The coming of the railways altered all this because the moderately affluent housekeeper of an average rural neighbourhood found it more profitable to do his shopping at the chief county town, or even in London, than at the nearest village shop or the nearest market town.

Writing in 1894, Jeaffreson remarks: "There is much fine talk nowadays in behalf of measures for reviving the old parochial life. What measures can revive a life that has lost irrecoverably all these fairly prosperous families?"

He then goes on about Woodbridge:

A more restful, sleepy, uneventful town of its size than the Woodbridge of to-day it would be difficult to find in all England. In the earlier decades of the Nineteenth century, from dawn to dusk the town was alive with stage-coaches driven by skilful whips, the private carriages of the great quality, and the post chaises of the rich traveller that passed through narrow Cumberland Street and the still narrower Thoroughfare of the quaint old town. Drawn by foaming four-in-hand teams, the stage coaches were attended by the rude but stirring music of the guard's horn. Drawn by the best posters of the road and guided by smartly equipt postillions, the chariots of the great were sometime preceded by outriders, wearing brave liveries.

He was a friend of FitzGerald, who spent so much time in Woodbridge because it reminded him of the Lynns and Carthews, the Moors and the Meadowses, the Nurseys of Bealings and the Woods of Melton.

Another feature of the Victorian countryside was the carrier. He finds such a large place in the directories, with "the places they go to, the inns they start from and the days of starting".

II

THE VILLAGE

····✿····

And hark! how blithe the throstle sings!
He too is no mean preacher:
Come forth into the light of things,
Let Nature be your teacher.
                              Wordsworth

So far we have dealt with the county as a whole, but a great deal
of an intimate nature can be obtained from local histories. A
particularly good one appeared from the pen of the Reverend
the Hon. A. F. Northcote on Monks Eleigh. He begins:

> The 19th., Century witnessed more important changes in Parish
> affairs than any that preceded it, at any rate since the 16th., century.
> When it opened the parish was a self-contained unit, it controlled its
> own poor, and its roads, it appointed its own constable; but it was
> not concerned with education, or with Public Health matters, such
> things were left to private effort. The sense of corporate responsi-
> bility had hardly dawned on poor people's minds, and the first
> action in the shape of New Poor Laws, proved to be the beginning
> of a new era in such matters. The abuses entailed by the expenditure
> of rates in aid of wages, and the incapacity of some parishes at any
> rate for dealing with the helpless poor, made reform a matter of
> necessity. [Vestries were brought to an end in 1894.]

There is a great deal of interesting information concerning
local affairs. For example, in 1837 there was such a deep snow, and
traffic was so much interrupted that farmers had to send their men
to clear the drifts, the cost of which amounted to £26 18s. 2½d.
This reminds us that there were particularly cold winters in 1859,
1860 and 1861.

The census returns from 1801 to 1901 for the village give a good
indication of how affairs were moving. The population in 1801

was 542, it rose with fair rapidity to the peak year, 1841, when the return was 733; it fell slowly during the next two decades, but made a little spurt in, or about, 1871, when 720 were recorded. This was due apparently to a fairly lively building and carpenter's shop in the village. After that numbers dropped steadily until 1901, when only 553 were recorded. The largest number of houses given as existing in the parish was 161 in 1861, and of these only 7 were empty. Judging from the register of baptisms entered, the peak decade again was 1832–41, when an average of 28·8 per year occurred, the first ten years, 1801–11 only showing an average of 17·4. After 1841 the numbers steadily fell, but in the later decades of the century more and more persons were baptized at the chapel. Of burials the same could be said, with interments in the chapel yard, but the earlier periods give a good idea of the mortality in the village. The peak years were the same; between 1831–51 the average number of burials was 15·1, and the three worst years were 1839 (26), 1840 (22) and 1841 (28). After 1851 figures dropped pretty steadily until the last decade, the average of church funerals was only 7·4.

One of the rectors took an interest in recording the causes of death in the margin of the register. Between April 1836 and July 1841, 102 burials were recorded and causes of death of 80 are given. Of these about 37 per cent were due to consumption or decline, 18 per cent to typhus fever, whilst the remaining 45 per cent were due to old age, accidents or other causes. Cancer claimed but two in the period.

The Reverend Northcote goes on: "In other ways things moved much as elsewhere, the larger population during the middle years indicated more labour in the fields, and better returns for the farmer, but the labourers' wages crept up only very slowly; it is true things got cheaper, and money went further, but there was room for improvement in conditions generally. During the last quarter of the century farming came in for a bad time, and values fell heavily in all ways; from an agricultural point of view one cannot end any record of that century with satisfaction."

In 1846 the parishioners decided to buy a fire engine, which was kept in a shed attached to the old workhouse and was to be for the use of the subscribers free of charge, to non-subscribers at a charge of £5. The engine was used occasionally as need arose,

but eventually was sold in 1874 for about £5 by order of the
vestry; there was some resentment felt about this action, as the
subscribers were not consulted and the engine did not belong to
the vestry.

Suffolk was then in the See of Norwich, with a small part in
Ely. The total number of cures was 522, derived from 324 rectories, 98 vicarages, 74 perpetual curacies and 26 chapelries. Of
these 138 were valued below £200 a year; 200 between £200
and £400 per annum; 111 from £400 to £600; 23, £600 to
£700; 12, £700 to £800; 7, £800 to £900; 5, £900 to £1,000
6, £1,000 to £1,200; 2, £1,200 to £1,500; and one, £1,500 to
£2,000. These were not the real values because one clergyman
declared that the estimates were usually one-third less than the
real income, and in some cases considerably more. Hitcham, a
Crown living, was valuable and was held for some time by Professor Henslow. Framlingham with Saxtead was the last on the
list, the richest of all.

In one parish the clergyman, a stout portly man, marched to
church in his surplice, smoking a long clay pipe. He returned to
the rectory in like manner. There were 90 licences for non-
residence, and only 86 parishes in which divine worship was
performed twice on Sundays. In several parishes services were held
only once a fortnight. In the Deanery of Samford, out of 28
parishes, five churches only were open for service twice on the
Sabbath. In 1854, no less than 48 Suffolk clergymen (20 in the
Eastern half and 28 in the Western), took out licences to kill game.

I have just come across one of these gentlemen, the Reverend
Christopher William Jeaffreson, M.A., Cantab., rector of Tun-
stall-cum-Dunningworth and of Iken. He was a tall man with a
handsome face and slightly aquiline profile, and was regarded as
the best partridge shot in East Suffolk. There was something
curious in the way he shot. It was his practice when he went out
with his gun and pointer to wear a waistcoat whose right-hand
pocket was lined with tinfoil and charged with snuff. As soon as
his dog had pointed, and he saw the covey on the point of rising,
he laid his gun on his left hand, forced the fingers of his right
hand into his snuff pouch, and took a pinch before he fired with
deadly effect at the birds on the wing. To enquirers who ques-
tioned his snuffing in this eccentric manner at a critical moment,

as to whether it was to clear his vision and steady his nerves, he would answer, "No. But I am so nervous and excitable that I am apt to fire before the birds have fairly risen, and to miss them by firing over their heads, unless I check my impetuosity by taking a hasty pinch."

The Reverend Robert Davers, who died in 1853, had held the living of Rougham since 1802, and also the rectory of St George, Bradfield, where he resided. The inhabitants of Rougham had in consequence, for about half a century, been without a resident incumbent. The living was worth about £800 a year. But the spiritual care of a thousand souls was left to a curate. The death of Mr Davers gave the opportunity of removing this blot upon the Establishment. But instead of placing at Rougham a young, earnest and high-principalled minister, the living was presented to the Reverend George Naylor, eighty-six years of age and made perfectly incompetent by his infirmities of discharging the pastoral duties. The Thirty-nine Articles had to be specially printed in Ipswich in large type to enable the aged minister to read them at his institution.

The income of these incumbents must be paralleled with those of the labourers, remembering the latter did not exceed 10s. weekly at this time. One wonders if these fat clerics took fees off these poor people when they came to be married or buried.

Many of the labourers were regular in attendance at church, but a large number became Dissenters, which was hardly to be wondered at. Generally speaking their attendance at church depended very much upon the attention paid to them by the clergyman of the parish.

If it was a period of long tenure in the Church, this was eclipsed by the doctors. Three generations of Worthingtons in a direct line practised at Lowestoft. They were of an ancient Suffolk family mentioned by Reyce in his *Breviary*. Then, there were no less than seven generations of Crowfoots at Beccles, but not necessarily in direct line.

But then associations went back such a long way, as witness the following which appeared about 1887: "Death of Margaret Catchpole's Friend and Companion. Mrs Elizabeth Abbott died at the house of her grandson at Wherstead Road on Thursday last at the advanced age of 105. Her father's name was Webb, lived in the parish of St. Clement and was in the employ of the Cobbold family. Taken to Trimley in infancy, then to domestic service in Ipswich when she became acquainted with Margaret Catchpole. They used to spend pleasant hours together on the banks of the Orwell. At 25 she married and went to London. When between 40 and 50, tramped from London to Ipswich carrying twins."

A large number of fairs still continued as a great attraction in the nineteenth century. Canon Raven noted as many as ninety-seven. Some were merely pleasure fairs, such as the one still held at Southwold on Trinity Monday. Others were for horses, cattle, cheese, wool, sheep, lambs, butter, hiring and pedlary. A great deal centred about Holy Thursday, Whit Monday and Old Michaelmas Day, 11th October.

Canon Raven writes:

Mildenhall Fair was held on Old Michaelmas Day, and a curious mixture it was of genuine business and spurious sausages, merry-go-rounds, ginger-bread, toys and crockery, rustic swains in velveteen-sleeved waistcoats adorned with a double row of mother-of-pearl buttons, apple-faced lassies with a profusion of ribbons, and alas! the kill-joy of the drinking booth with a squeaky fiddle to invite to jollity. One of these noble institutions bore the legend:

> Rove not from Booth to Booth,
>   But step in Here;
> Nothing Excel [sic] the music
>   But the Beer.

He goes on to say that his mother used to buy her knives at a Sheffield stall, and replenish her broken crockery at another. "The fair has passed away. It was even in its decay serving important commercial purposes after a primitive fashion, as any one would say who saw Barrett's china-men from Cambridge, turning out of the empty crates in which they had slept on a fine autumn morning."

Another writer bemoaned the habits that accompanied the private sale of stock—the wasted hours; the gin and beer for the pig dealers; the dinner, lasting hours for the lamb buyers; the spirits or wine for the bullocks, sheep and wool buyers. And the negotiations often from noon to night possibly without success.

The nineteenth century must have seen the gardens of the great houses in their utmost perfection. It should be remembered that 1854 saw the advent into England of the Maréchal Niel Rose, through Cant's famous nurseries in Colchester, in company with the Gloire de Dijon. China roses of all varieties were greatly used, some being perfected into rose hedges.

Shrubland Hall was one of the most noted, with its Italianate gardens, its site the finest of any house in Suffolk. The ground lent itself to terracing, and terraced it was, with the utmost splendour of material, design and decoration. A flag was flown when the occupants were in residence, and the Prince Consort once paid it a visit. (It is a curious fact that Queen Victoria never once set foot in the county.)

The staff employed there numbered 173; made up of indoor 17, stables 16, keepers and night men 16, warreners 4, parks 10, gardeners 40, lodge keepers 3, blacksmiths 2, carpenters 7, painters 3, engineers 2, home farm 38, brick kilns 9, bricklayers 4, wheelwrights 2.

Sudbourne Hall was the centre of one of the most remarkable sporting estates in England. It was described as a kind of Beaulieu plus Holkham. Its marshes, full of wild fowl and hares, recalled Lord Leicester's great Norfolk seat, though the decoy at Holkham was disused, whilst that at Iken was in full working order. The estate covered more than 20 square miles and was bordered on three sides by tidal rivers, which made it a kind of separate area of Suffolk. In front, seawards, the Ore came down south from Aldeburgh and ran mile after mile, skirting Sudbourne and Orford, parallel with the great shingle bank and the sea. This was joined on the south by the Butley river. In fact the estate formed a peninsula, entered only from the land at the back, over the wild and picturesque uplands of Tunstall Heath.

The house was sold by the Marquis of Hertford to Sir Richard Wallace in 1871. The garden was laid out in 1872, and the conservatories erected. It was sold again in 1884 and again in 1897. A few of the fine pollarded oaks, the peculiar product of this part of Suffolk, ornamented the banks of the lake. The lawn was mowed by two steam mowers. Above the roses were the aviaries, where the famous Sudbourne Eagle was kept. A white-tailed eagle, it was caught in the early '70s in a trap, but was not injured. There was also an octagonal game-house of two stories that had accommodation for 4,000 head at one time.

It was interesting to discover that Beatrix Potter visited Melford Hall, with its beautiful garden, to see her cousins the Hyde Parkers. On leaving, she left one of her inimitable sketches on the dressing table. It was of Mr Rat reclining in a four-poster bed with his tail trailing out at the bottom. She must have been rather young when she did this, because the tail comes out from under the mattress rather than on top.

Sanitation in those days was none too good, and one comes across letters such as the following in high-class publications: "Can you or any of your readers advise me of an effectual way of getting rid of house beetles? We are very much troubled with these?" The answer was: "Sprinkle the floor liberally with Keating's powder every night." One should not forget, however, that fleas and bugs were in palaces as well as cottage homes.

Then comes this, reminder of the way in which poor horses were plagued: "There are at present thousands of flies in my stables and saddle room. During the day they are a terrible nuisance to both horse and man, and towards evening they settle in large black patches on the ceilings and walls." Those were the days when a man had his favourite horse's hoofs made into ink pots, for his study table.

A notable little book was produced in 1870 by an Aldeburgh doctor, N. F. Hele. It throws a very direct light on the habits of nature lovers of those times. He notes that a rush was very abundant about the fen and mere. It was used for litter, and a few people at Aldringham collected and prepared it for rushlight wicks. Coarse door mats were made at Thorpe and elsewhere of the blades and stem of the common *Arunda arenaria*. (My mother used to make and trim the rushlights as a child, and my grand-father could make the door mats.)

He then proceeds to give expression of love for birds:

Rare birds do occasionally put in here, as for instance an Avocet which was killed some years ago by a friend. Some of the Marsh Hawks are generally to be seen, but only occasionally shot, there being no means of concealment.

Coldfairgreen, Erne or white-tailed eagle shot. Fine specimen of rough-legged Buzzard killed, Nov. 5. 1865.

The Iceland Falcon. A specimen of this beautiful bird was killed at Sudbourne, October 14, 1867. The Peregrine Falcon, killed August 14, 1864. Montagu's Harrier, killed today, May 14, 1868 on the Mere at Thorpe.

The raven. Two have taken up their quarters in a little wood near Thorpe, by the water mill; but will not allow the least chance of a shot. I have been after them morning after morning for several days past; and although concealing myself, they will not come within range, but soar overhead at a great height, uttering their well known "Cronk! cronk!"

Night Jar. September 29, 1861, whilst driving to Leiston to-day I met with one of these birds, asleep on the bough of a fir tree, and killed it with my whip.

A wearisome list of slaughter of rare species, often for the mere lust of shooting. It is to be hoped that his gun was buried with him. He mentions that the red-legged partridge was introduced by the Marquis of Hertford. He also refers to the large quantities of coprolites that were obtained from Orford, Chilsford [sic], and Butley. This brings to mind that Suffolk was in the van for scientific farming.

Coprolites were first discovered on a farm at Levington in the eighteenth century, but it was Professor Henslow who first discovered this fossilized substance in the cliffs at Bawdsey and Felixstowe. He communicated with J. B. Lawes of Rothamsted, who in 1843 was working with Edward Packard, dissolving bones in acid with a view to producing a fertilizer. Eventually Packard had a small works for grinding coprolites at Snape in 1843, and in 1854 he erected a complete superphosphate factory and sulphuric acid works at Bramford. Joseph Fison had a similar business in Ipswich. It is a curious fact that these coprolite pits, of which there were so many, employing many men who became known as "Old Coproliters", folded up almost as by common consent about 1893.

The sugar beet industry was started at Lavenham in 1869 by a Mr James Duncan, but was forced to close down in 1873 for lack of support. And this is what the *Food Journal* said at the time:

In 1868 Mr. James Duncan, a merchant of Mincing Lane, determined to try if he could not establish some method of encouraging the English cultivation of the [beet] root, and of making sugar from it, and with great pluck and spirit erected a sugar factory at Lavenham, in Suffolk, at a considerable expense hoping thereby to induce farmers in the neighbourhood to grow the needful supplies. They showed very little hesitation at falling in with his plans, and such success has attended the movement, that the whole district has felt the benefit. Formerly, the farmer grew but little beet-root, and what he did grow was for the purpose of feeding—for conversion into beef; mangold, however, at 7/6 per ton profit, was the article commonly used for the cattle, the beet being a little more valuable on account of its high proportion of sugar. But now the Farmer takes his load of beet to the sugar factory, and there is paid 20/- a ton—a clear gain of one half—and, in addition to that, instead of returning empty, he brings back a load of pulp or beet bread, the very essence of the feeding material, for which he pays 12/- a ton, thus obtaining superior nourishment for his cattle. As the soil of Lavenham appears exceedingly well suited for the root, producing on an average 30 tons an acre, the farmers are naturally delighted with their steady outlet for their produce, and each year sees a fresh lot of beet-root grown.

Home brewing was the order of the day, always it would seem the prerogative of the woman. She had a wonderful sense in her fingers when dealing with sweet wort, as also in working the old brick ovens. Rain-water was considered best, but one brew would differ from another in its glory. A mug of beer was acceptable as a reward for a service rendered, and a niggard might be referred to in the oblique manner thus: "If anyone ax yow where I bin tu, yew can saay I bin tu Mr Whelpuns. Should any one ax yow what sort o' beer he brew yew can saay, I doan't know."

Richard Garrett in 1849 wrote from Leiston to the Agricultural Society on the matter of obtaining a good beer for his people; the spelling is his:

I intend to wait on your Lordship some early day to explain my idea of the necessity (to prevent monopoly) of Lisencing another public house in this village. We are most grossly imposed upon by the only house there is at present in this parish being illibrally tied too & supplied very badly by its present owner, a brewer, wine, spirit & cigar merchant & my business, its visitors & the workmen I employ are so badly served that I consider it my duty to beg your Lordship's kind assistance in lisencing another house

Steer and stockman about 1895

'The Feathers', Walton, Felixstowe

Dressed for the occasion and photographed at Ipswich

Old Bolton, Ipswich, 1881, from a painting by Robert Burrows

forthwith so they can be supplied with good articles at reasonable prices.

My Lord,
Your mo. obt. & very
Faithful sert.
Rd. Garrett.

And it was a Suffolk man, from Bawdsey, who was to become known as the apostle of pure beer, with reference to which this appeared in *Country Life*, for 22nd December 1900:

Whether arsenical beer poisoning comes from foreign material used in the manufacture of the beer, or from india rubber tubes used when beer is drawn by the horrible, but almost universally used pumps, it is plain that the Pure Beer Movement has received a great stimulus, and it is probable that a great triumph is awaiting for Sir Cuthbert Quilter. All over the Country the farmers, especially those who can grow barley of good malting sample, are agitating in the matter; and we wish them well, for English agriculture is not so prosperous that a fillip will do it any harm. Our fear is that the genuine beer may prove less palatable to vitiated palates than the liquid which is now commonly drunk.

Yet this village life, restricted as it was, was full of happiness. It engendered a great pride of place and workmanship. Suffolk men in an age that was quick with life, had built those marvellous churches; Suffolk straw and reed thatched the roofs; Suffolk horses pulled the ploughs; Suffolk earth made the walls, the old red tiles, even the pots and pans in constant use. And it was into their native Suffolk soil they were gathered to their fathers, whose pattern they had followed so faithfully.

THE TOWNS

―――――――――――――――・・✤・・――――――――――――――

> 'Twas town, yet country too; you felt the warmth
> Of clustering houses in the wintry time;
> Supped with a friend, and went by lantern home.
> Yet from your chamber window you could hear
> The tiny bleat of new-yeaned lambs, or see
> The children bend beside the hedgerow banks
> To pluck the primroses.

"The County town, Ipswich, exhibits the representation of a Village in its churches and chapels; of the Town, in its markets; of the County Town, in its prison and courts of justice; of the Sea Port, in its tidal river and dock; of the Site of Artisanship, in its varied manufactures; and its philanthropic character in its public buildings and charitable associations." So wrote John Glyde in 1856; and a better picture of a small market town, with a newly arrived railway could hardly be drawn. But Ipswich was growing fast, although many people in Suffolk villages at those times had never travelled so far, with the exception of one or two enterprising souls who may have walked there. For that matter many of them had never seen the sea, which was then known as the German Ocean, or the German Sea; and Lowestoft Ness to seaman was "Abraham's Bosom". The first mayor was Mr B. Brame, who took office in 1836.

When Queen Victoria came to the throne, Ipswich was essentially an agricultural town, set in the midst of cornfields and orchards, with narrow streets that hardly allowed space on each side of the road for people to walk uninterruptedly if a tumbrel went by. A river ran along one side of it, and met the tide from the estuary of the Orwell, just as it had done for centuries.

"At that time", wrote a native, "if you walked down Fore

Street, St. Clement's, and entered any of the merchants' yards on the right, you were almost at the river's edge. The warehouses themselves were on a line with the river, and in many places, not even a rat could run along without tumbling into the water."

Stoke Hills was a favourite rambling place for Ipswich boys. Angelsea Road was the favourite country lane walk from the Norwich Road to old Tacket Street Chapel, with green hedges and pollard oaks. Fonnereau Road was merely a footpath, with hawthorn hedges on each side. Berners Street, Orford Street, High Street, with all the intermediate streets connecting them were either gardens or ploughed fields.

The pleasure grounds enjoyed by the inhabitants at the beginning of the reign and until near its end, were the woods and heathlands, and the river banks. Hog Highland was one of the popular places of resort on high days and holidays, varied by visits to Freston Woods, the banks and also the waters of the Gipping, and a stroll along the Strand on the road to Freston. Nearer at hand was the Promenade, in the neighbourhood of the Dock, a shady place in summer days between the rows of limes, which led to 'The Umbrella', a small sort of summerhouse, from which a view could be obtained down the river across the Cliff Bight.

Conditions were indeed primitive. Old people could remember a tobacco-cutting machine belonging to Churchman's, that was worked by a horse walking round in a circle in a half-open yard. The Fleece Inn was the scene of the last bull-baiting in the town. Some of the old shops in Northgate Street you either went down into or up into. Wombwell's Menagerie exhibited on Cornhill, when St George's Fair was a three-day annual event. Many of the main streets were cobbled. But during the year ending July 1852 there were 6,130 loads of stone and 122 loads of broken granite laid on the roads of Ipswich.

Then John Glyde reports this in 1850: "The town is lighted by 228 gas lamps and 10 oil lamps. These are placed at various distances from each other. The average distance apart of the gas lamps is 87 yards, of the oil lamps 146 yards; but at the present time in placing fresh lamps, a space of 60 yards is the utmost distance allowed between two lights. No less than 60 streets are without lamps."

Some idea of the sanitary condition of the town can be gleaned by an extract from the report made in 1848 by Mr Austin, civil engineer to the local authority. It was stated that "practically Ipswich was without any system of sewerage. Of sewers for the accommodation of the drainage of houses there was none; they either drain to cesspools and dead wells or not at all. The slops and refuse being thrown into the streets and the foundations of the town saturated with foul and pestilential moisture." The built-in area in those days was very limited and in fact only covered the lower parts around the docks and the Orwell. When the dock was constructed it became necessary to intercept the drain which discharged into the river, and what is known as the dock sewer was constructed with outlets at St Peter's Dock and near the present Ship Launch Road. The low-level sewer was constructed in 1882.

The Ipswich Dock Act was passed in 1837, and the foundation stone of the lock was laid in June 1839. Then, in November 1841, the first ship entered through the lock gate on the west side. The dock was formed by cutting off an L-shaped portion of the old river bed, building embankments at both ends, and making a channel, still called the 'New Cut', on the west side to take the water from the Gipping farther down the main stream. At the date of completion the dock had an area of 33 acres, and was the largest wet dock in the kingdom.

In order to give a better approach to the dock, however, a new entrance lock 300 feet long and 50 feet wide, and having a depth of water of 23 feet 6 inches at average high-water tides was constructed at the southern end in 1881; the lock gates and gears being made by Messrs E. R. and F. Turner at St Peter's Works. As the dredging of the river had been carried out almost continuously from the time of the formation of the commission, the navigable channel now permitted vessels of 2,000 tons to enter the dock.

This is what Glyde said about it: "Below the wet dock, the river Gipping joins the Orwell, which expands into a broad estuary, in which the tide rises about 14 feet. When viewed at full tide this may be pronounced one of the finest salt water rivers in England. The rising land is clothed with noble avenues of trees and a rich luxuriancy of wood, adorned with fine mansions, farm houses and village churches."

In 1830 the protection of the town against fire was in the hands of the Suffolk Alliance Fire Office, which maintained two large and three smaller manuals, one kept by the police. The staff consisted of a superintendent—whose duties, for which he was paid £20 per annum, were part-time—and twenty-eight men. They were aided at big conflagrations by others who were attracted to the scene. The town council took over in 1875, and in 1884 the first steam-driven pump of 250–300 gallons capacity was purchased. In 1899 a second pump of 450 gallons was added, and the fire station moved from Waterworks Street to Bond Street.

A provisional order to provide horse-drawn trams was obtained by a private company in 1879, and the first of these was running from the Cornhill via Princes Street to the station in 1880.

The first East Suffolk and Ipswich Hospital was opened in 1836, and Dr A. H. Bartlet was the first honorary surgeon. He was succeeded by his son, Dr J. H. Bartlet. The first treasurer and secretary was Mr John Chevallier Cobbold, who was succeeded in turn by his son, Mr John Patteson Cobbold. This meant that two doctors and two treasurers held office for nearly a century.

When Mr John Prior succeeded Mr Fitch as postmaster in 1867 there were about twenty-five persons of all grades employed on the staff. The Corporation Museum originated in a society founded in 1846 to provide a museum for the instruction of the working classes in natural history. This was opened in Museum Street in 1847. The borough was one of the first to adopt the Public Libraries Act, and a small reference collection was formed in connection with the museum in 1852. The lending library was built as a Jubilee memorial in 1887. The corn exchange was opened in 1882. In fact nearly all modern Ipswich was built within the lifetime of men then living. One thing more, 1868 was the year of the last open election.

In 1841 Ransomes, Sims and Jefferies exhibited at the Liverpool Show of the Royal Agricultural Society of England a portable steam engine for agricultural purposes, and at Bristol in the following year they showed the same engine made self-moving—in other words, a traction engine. This had a short vertical boiler in the front with the engine behind, and a platform at the rear to carry the thrashing machine which it was to drive.

The firm of E. R. and F. Turner was founded in July 1837, and began its activities as iron founders and general engineers in St Peter's Works, alongside the Wolsey Gate in College Street. Its foundation coincided more or less with the commencement of the industrial development of Ipswich. At first they made stone mills, horse gear and cake breakers, and a small steam engine.

And this from Clarke's Ipswich, so characteristic of those early Victorian dresses: "There is a manufactory for stays, by Messrs Edwards, which is deserving of every encouragement, as upwards of seven hundred women and girls are engaged."

M. Betham-Edwards in her book *Reminiscences*, gives a vivid picture of those early days. She was then living at Westerfield and about 12 years old. "Walking one day to Ipswich, we met a labourer's wife and her daughters, girls of twelve and fourteen.

" 'So, Mrs. P—' said my elder sister, 'you have been shopping?' "

" 'No, Miss,' replied the good woman with an unmistakable air of self approval, 'but I am anxious to do my girls all the good I can, so I have just taken them to see a man hanged.' "

She also mentions the butter market being held on a Saturday, and a certain rosy-cheeked, blue-eyed old dame jogging there in a donkey cart. When she had sold her butter and eggs, she used to bring back books and parcels. "With what excitement I caught sight of the donkey cart halting by our garden gate."

Bury St Edmunds, also known as the Montpelier of England.

Bury must always have been a delightful country town, and is justly and completely expressed in the motto of its coat of arms: *Sacrarium Regis, Cunabula Legis* (The Shrine of the King, the Cradle of the Law). Its history hangs about its once-magnificent abbey, founded in the seventh century, which drew all men's feet to its wealth and splendour. But as this book deals with Victorian Suffolk, we might approach the town by the familiar words of one who gave readings from his works in the Athenaeum, and must have enjoyed his stay there very much indeed: Charles Dickens in *Pickwick Papers*.

"Beg your pardon, sir," said Sam ". . . Is this Bury St. Edmunds?"
"It is," replied Mr. Pickwick.
The coach rattled through the well-paved streets of a handsome little town, of thriving and cleanly appearance, and stopped before a

large inn, situated in a wide open street, nearly facing the old
abbey.

"And this," said Mr. Pickwick looking up, "is the Angel! We
alight here, Sam."

It was here that Sam was to meet with considerable adventure.

Early on the ensuing morning, Mr. Weller was dispelling all the
feverish remains of the previous evening's conviviality, through the
instrumentality of a halfpenny shower-bath (having induced a
young gentleman attached to the stable department, by the offer of
that coin, to pump over his head and face until he was perfectly
restored), when he was attracted by the appearance of a young
fellow in mulberry-coloured livery, who was sitting on a bench in
the yard, reading what appeared to be a hymnbook, with an air of
deep abstraction, but who occasionally stole a glance at the individual
under the pump, as if he took some interest in the proceedings,
nevertheless.

There was also the incident of Mr Pickwick lying in ambush
at the young ladies' academy, when he was spied by an inquisitive
boarder through the hinge of the door. But Bury youths in those
days were fond of a joke, and one of their favourites was to
remove the sign of the Black Boy Inn during the night, and re-
erect it on the front of a select academy for young ladies. This
may well have been the very one which raised so much gallantry
in Mr Pickwick.

It was on this Angel Hill that the famous Bury Fair was held.
From 29th September to 5th November it became an old-
fashioned country fair, and almost the whole space from the
Athenaeum to the corner of Northgate Street was filled with
stalls and booths of various descriptions, from the humble ginger-
bread stall to the more imposing theatre, where the legitimate
drama was presented in the form of blood-curdling tragedies
about every half hour.

Victorian respectability was credited with being the ultimate
factor which killed not only the Bury Fair but also similar
institutions in 1872. Show people who came into the town were
blamed for bringing in smallpox and typhus. A petition to end
what had been a nuisance was made in 1866.

To the Worshipful the Mayor and Corporation of Bury St.
Edmunds. We the undersigned, beg to call your serious attention to

the nuisance and dangers which are inflicted upon the residents of the town and neighbourhood by the annual Fair, held on Angel Hill, and we venture to urge upon you the necessity of forthwith putting an end to a state of things which is a disgrace to the County, and a scandal to the age. We believe that no valid ground can be brought forward in favour of its continuance, and we present the following as amongst the most obvious arguments for its abolition:

    1.—It has become useless and unnecessary.
    2.—It is a source of danger to the public.
    3.—It demoralises the population in town and country.

This brings to mind that the county council was set up in 1889. Until then magistrates had run West Suffolk's business.

Public houses in the Mildenhall area in 1872, were open at 5 a.m. and closed at 11 p.m. and one of these inns was called the 'Kicking Dickey'. Bury had five brewers in 1855, ten maltsters and six coopers. The brewery draymen had to be home by seven o'clock. In addition many public houses brewed their own beer, so did many landowners and the bigger farmers. There were even breweries in some of the villages. It was said that one of the big items of expense in fighting fires was the cost of supplying beer to the thirsty firemen. Great Barton children were given half a pint of beer each on St Valentine's Day, by a Mrs Payne of Elm Farm, when they went round saying their pieces. And the election of 1857 was described as the dryest ever known in the town.

Another item in the drinking line was held at Everard's Hotel in 1886, when Mr H. Lacey Scott sold by auction about 200 dozen of wines made by the late Mr John Darkin of St Peter's Vineyard. The red wine, of 1873 vintage, made from 26s. per dozen downwards.

And this from Tymm's *Handbook*: "Vinery, Out Westgate. The grounds of Mr. J. A. Darkin are so favourably situated as to aspect and locality that he has succeeded in growing to perfection in the open air several varieties of foreign grapes, which challenge comparison with those imported. The spot is a sunny slope near the hospital, sheltered from the north winds by a wall 22 feet high, and a hill behind of gradual incline to a height of 90 feet."

Bury was thoughtful of its old war veterans. The town's few surviving Waterloo veterans were entertained by their friends to dinner at the White Horse Inn in June 1858 in celebration of the victory. The last veteran died in 1868 aged 80. Hundreds of pounds were raised in 1857 to help the victims of the Indian Mutiny. A Norton soldier who had lost an arm at the Battle of the Alma was appointed letter carrier from Woolpit to Felsham.

The last public execution took place in 1851, when George Carnt, who had murdered a girl at Lawshall, was hanged in the presence of 5,000 people. He was said to have given rise to the expression: "Don't say carnt. Carnt is dead." With the usual hunting after mementoes, in 1886 the rope with which Catherine Foster was hanged in 1847 for poisoning her husband was offered for sale. It fetched 3s. It was sold by a former turnkey at the county gaol.

There was also the usual petty thefts that were suitably magnified. For example five little boys were charged before the mayor with carrot stealing off the land in the occupation of G. H. Nunn of Eldo House. As they pleaded want, and appeared very penitent, they were at the kind suggestion of the prosecution dismissed with a warning.

Then, on Saturday night or early Sunday morning last (July 1855), some person or persons entered the enclosed garden of the Reverend H. G. Hand at Hepworth Rectory and stole some cucumbers and lettuce. Of course, they may have had them for Sunday tea. But he was not the incumbent who went to his Sunday duties on horseback and stabled his horse in the vestry. It could be heard neighing its responses during the service. That was a memory that belonged to old people at Great Barton.

Naturally enough there was witchcraft in Bury in 1855. A boy of 12 who lived in Churchgate Street, was made to dance for three hours by his family in the hope that his attacks of St Vitus' Dance would be cured. His parents had been advised by a local wise woman that the only remedy lay in charming away his troubles. And a woman at Norton was widely believed to put spells on people.

For many years during the nineteenth century Bury St Edmunds and Mildenhall were supplied with coal and other heavy goods by means of the river Lark. At Bury barges left the river at Fornham St Martin church, entered an artificial canal (known as the Coal River), and were unloaded at a wharf against the old maltings on the Mildenhall Road.

Turning to manufactures, Robert Boby's in 1887 produced dressing machines (fitted with blowers to free the grain from dust), haymakers' horse-rakes and barley hummellers (these were to remove the awms from the grain). In this first year, 1856, 200 corn-screens were made. The business was started in an iron-monger's shop.

In 1855, Mr George T. Bloomfield, a Thelnethan millwright and engineer, introduced several improvements in a steam threshing engine which he made. It threshed a stout crop of mown wheat, the produce of 10 acres, in a fair day's work, and with a small consumption of coal.

One or two little internal affairs are not without interest. On 14th July 1855 Thomas Francis Lucia brought out the first copy of the *Bury Free Press* (that is free of stamp duty) in a shed in a back garden just off High Baxter Street. One of the advertisements which appeared in its early years was by a Mr Matthews in St Andrew's Street, who offered to take daguerreotype portraits, from half-a-crown each complete with frame.

In 1868 the doors of the houses were numbered by the Paving Commission. Many people objected, and one old lady 'bested' them as only a good old Suffolker could. As soon as the painter's back was turned she popped out and rubbed the nasty 'owd' thing off her door. Other residents warned the painter off and threatened to prosecute him. Then, coming down the years, a system of refuse collecting was introduced in 1880.

"Mr Charles Dickens will read at the Athenaeum Hall on Thursday evening October, 13, 1859, his *Christmas Carol*, and 'Trial from Pickwick', The reading will last two hours and twenty minutes." He also read from *David Copperfield* in October 1861. Charles Kingsley lectured at the Athenaeum in January 1857 on the "Pleasures and Adventures of the Study of Natural History".

Turning to Mildenhall, the school there was founded and maintained by the Bunbury family. For many years Lady Bunbury gave prizes at the Flower Show for the best kept donkeys in the parish. A woman died there of cholera in 1854.

But I have kept the best thing to the last, viz. the famous King Edward's School, founded in 1550 by Edward VI and sometimes known as the Eton of East Anglia. It had a great record which shone brilliantly in the Victorian years, through head masters and pupils. Its three hundredth anniversary was celebrated on 2nd August 1850, with a sermon preached in St James' Church by Dr Blomfield, Bishop of London, who was a former old boy. Then in April 1883 the school was removed to the vineyard of the old abbey. The school has always been of the highest repute.

However, we will leave this splendid little town celebrating the old Queen's Jubilee of 1887, when 1,575 plum puddings and 2,480 pounds of beef were given away. Perhaps the feast was held in the streets, at long tables, as at Saxmundham. Or maybe, it was on the great meeting centre of Angel Hill.

Stowmarket was described as a clean and healthy market town; and so it was, situated at the junction of three rivulets that formed the river Gipping. It was governed by a local board of health, and was well lighted with gas.

In the 1879 Directory we are informed that a considerable trade in corn, malt, coal, slate and timber was carried on. Messrs Lankester and Wells had extensive wine vaults and were the proprietors of the bonding warehouse, the first established under the Inland Revenue in the eastern counties.

A horticultural show was held in July, for fruit, flowers and vegetables, and prizes given for the six best cultivated cottagers' gardens within 6 miles of the town. Amongst the private residents was a Miss Purr, surely a lovely name for a single woman.

Amongst the commercial gentlemen was a John Hayward; solicitor; commissioner of oaths; clerk to the directors and guardians of Old Stow hundred; steward of Eton College Suffolk manors, and the manors of Thorney-Lezons, Thorney-Mumpliers, with Braziers and Earl Stonham; commissioner of land tax for the hundred of Bosmere and Claydon.

Mrs Catherine Olive Fison was a manufacturer of improved kiln tiles, maltster, miller, wool merchant, and brick and tile manufacturer in Finborough Road. But the way things were mixed up in the most inconsequential manner was somewhat alarming. For instance, Robert Barker was a general smith, machinist, agricultural implement agent and a pork butcher. Woods, Cocksedge and Company were engineers, manufacturers of general agricultural, hydraulic and steam machinery, millwrights, wagon and cart builders. But surely the most significant business was that of the Patent Safety Gun Cotton Company.

Probably the greatest event in the life of Stowmarket was the great explosion on Friday, 11th August 1871 which shook all Suffolk. This occurred at the Guncotton Works, when twenty-four people were killed—eleven men, seven boys and six girls; and fifty-seven were injured. The explosion rocked buildings within an 11-mile radius and was heard more than 20 miles away. Five of the girls were blown into such minute fragments that no identifiable trace of them was ever found. A tragic feature of the disaster was that many of the dead workers were young children who nowadays would be at school.

The explosion occurred at five minutes past two o'clock, just after the 120 employees had returned from the dinner hour. In an instant every window of that part of Stowmarket was shattered, roofs were stripped off, and one large house on the Ipswich Road, completely wrecked. The first explosion was followed by a fire which swept through the wreckage of the factory.

At 3 p.m. there was a second, though less violent explosion, which killed the two proprietors, the brothers Edward and William Prentice, while they were leading a frantic endeavour to save people trapped in the ruins. Both were blown to pieces. One of Edward Prentice's legs, picked up a long way from the scene, was identified as part of his body by a sock.

In those days guncotton was a comparatively new explosive, and the Stowmarket Works, established in 1863, was the only factory in the world producing it.

The inquest dragged on for weeks, but eventually the jury decided that the explosion was caused by some person, or persons unknown, adding sulphuric acid to the guncotton after it had passed the final safety test before being sent out from the factory.

The Sunday after, 20,000 people flocked into the little town, making a holiday of it, some even becoming intoxicated.

One of the juvenile members of the Prentice family wrote this in her diary, she was then 13: "This has been the most terrible day in our lives. Mama is prostrate with grief and Papa saw William [her brother] blown to pieces and Edward too. William had only just arrived from Heidelberg University and had called to see Papa before coming here. All laughter has left our home. Will dear Papa ever smile again, I wonder? His sadness enfolds us all."

IV

SOME EMINENT SUFFOLK VICTORIANS

················❦··············

The chief glory of every people arises from its authors.

Johnson

It would be interesting to know who were the two authors returned in the 1851 census, because the county could surely boast rather more than that. For example, there was Alfred Inigo Suckling, 1796–1856. He was the son of Alexander Fox of Norwich, and his mother's name was Anna Maria Suckling. He eventually assumed his mother's maiden name and thus succeeded to the Suckling estates and coat of arms. His *History of Suffolk* ran to two volumes but was never completed.

Bernard Barton, 1764–1849, became the Woodbridge Poet. He was a contributor to *Household Words* and attracted the notice of Sir Robert Peel, who procured him an annual pension.

Barton was born in London of Quaker parents, but educated at a Quaker school at Ipswich. Apprenticed to a tradesman at Halstead, Essex, he married the daughter. Next he went into partnership with a Mr Jessup at Woodbridge, and set up as a corn and coal merchant. He finally became a clerk in the Quaker bank of Alexander and Company, of Woodbridge, where he remained until his death. He was a great friend of FitzGerald, who most ill-advisedly married his daughter. And also of Charles Lamb, who gave him such excellent but whimsical advice. This is what FitzGerald said of him: "Few, high or low, but were glad to see him at his customary place in the bank from which he smiled a kindly greeting, or came down with friendly open hand and some frank words of family enquiry—perhaps with the offer of a pinch from his never failing snuff-box."

Agnes Strickland, 1806–74, was a member of a gifted family who lived at Reydon Hall, near Southwold. She wrote the *Lives of the Queens of England* in twelve volumes, published in 1848. It was really a joint work with her sister Elizabeth, who refused to be named on the title page. Agnes could be seen often driving in Southwold, wearing her gold rings over her gloved fingers. She is buried in Southwold churchyard.

Edward FitzGerald, 1809–83, was born at Bredfield and educated at the famous Bury School. He was faithful all his life to Suffolk, and never long absent, a lonely, shy, kind-hearted man. He was gifted with singular powers of winning affection, in spite of eccentric and recluse habits, and it was said he was the only acquaintance with whom George Borrow did not quarrel. His literary fame rests on the *Rubaiyat*. He also contributed "Sea Words and Phrases Along the Suffolk Coast", which appeared in early numbers of the *East Anglian Notes and Queries*.

In February 1972, a representative of His Excellency the Persian Ambassador planted six rose trees around FitzGerald's grave in Boulge churchyard. They had been sent from Iran. A service was held by the Rector. Lines from the *Rubaiyat* were read and children from nearby schools gathered round the grave with its simple inscription: "It is He that hath made us, and not we ourselves." Representatives of the Omar Khayyam Club were also present. The Persian Embassy had donated the plants as part of their 2,500th celebration of the Persian Empire—the year of Cyrus the Great.

This was a most happy occasion, reminiscent of the one inscribed on the small iron plate on the grave:

"This Rose Tree Raised in Kew Gardens from Seed Brought by William Simpson Artist-Traveller from the Grave of Omar Khayyam at Naishapur was Planted by a few Admirers of Edward FitzGerald in the name of the Omar Khayyam Club. 7th October, 1893."

Charles Montagu Doughty, 1843–1926, was an English travel writer and poet. He was born at Theberton Hall and studied at Caius College, Cambridge. Out of two years' travel and hardship in Arabia (1875–7), slowly grew his great book *Travels in Arabia Deserta*, published 1888. It was described as a prose classic.

Marie Louise de la Ramee, 1839–1908, who adopted the pen name of Ouida, was born at Bury St Edmunds of a supposed

French refugee, but early emigrated to Italy where much of her work was done.

Orlando Whistlecraft was buried at Thwaite under the simple inscription of "Weather Prophet and Poet. Born 1810, died 1893." He was described as the 'Suffolk Meteorologist', and his industry and care, exercised for many years, stored up valuable information for which he did not receive the reward due to his observations and labours. He gave the following country calendar: "The Daisy opens in February; Lesser Celandine in March; Water Crowfoot in April; Meadow Crowfoot in May; Speedwell about May 7; Cuckoo arrives—April 16; Nightingale, April 25; Swallow April 16; House Martin, April 20; Redstart, April 20; Wryneck, April 10; Soaring of the Lark, March 22." This calls to mind Meredith's "Lark Ascending":

> For singing till his heaven fills,
> 'Tis love of earth that he instils,
> And ever winging up and up,
> Our valley is his golden cup,
> And he the wine that overflows
> To lift us with him as he goes.

Sir John Cordy Burrows, F.R.C.S., 1813–76, was born at Ipswich, where he attended the grammar school. He was one of the makers of Victorian Brighton, where he practised. He was instrumental in establishing the public library, museum and picture gallery, and he advocated the incorporation of the town and the purchase of the now much-esteemed Pavilion.

Sir William Jackson Hooker and Joseph Dalton Hooker his son, lived at Halesworth. The son was a friend and fellow worker with Darwin.

Prince Dhuleep Singh, G.C.S.I., 1838–93, purchased Elveden Hall in 1863. He was familiarly known as the Black Prince, became a country squire and was much interested in local archaeology.

Although Elizabeth Garrett Anderson was born in London in 1836, she was a typical Suffolk Victorian. Her father Newson Garrett was back in his native county in 1841, having brought his wife and four children in a hoy, landing at Slaughden Quay. His father, Richard Garrett, the ironmonger of Leiston had died in 1837, but the business passed to his brother, another Richard.

Newson was to create the famous malting and coal industry at Snape. Unfortunately Newson's life was a series of feuds and upheavals with his neighbours. But it was his spirit that enabled Elizabeth to pass through the then only open door into the stronghold of masculine faculty, that of the Society of Apothecaries. When the society realized what the young woman was after, they tried hard to close the narrow opening in her face, but her father would have none of it, and she graduated as the first English-trained woman doctor. She was to become the first woman dean of a medical school, as later in her retirement the first woman mayor.

When Elizabeth was 13 and her sister 15, they were sent to a boarding school for ladies kept by the Misses Browning at Blackheath. They were aunts to the poet Robert Browning. But Elizabeth, a strong-willed and demanding pupil, did not fit into the scheme of things. Newson decided to take all the extras for his daughters, including one more, viz. a hot bath once a week. That was an almost unheard of thing in those days of no bathrooms. Accordingly the wooden washtub was placed before the kitchen range, surrounded by towels, and the two girls became known as 'the bathing Garretts'.

It was not until I read Jo Manton's biography of Elizabeth that I realized what a struggle Elizabeth had to become a doctor, and what were the dreadful horrors of a Victorian operating theatre in the days of pre-Lister surgery.

John Cordy Jeaffreson, 1831–1901, British author and archivist, was born at Framlingham, and educated at grammar schools at Woodbridge and Botesdale; also at Pembroke College, Oxford. He was for a time a private tutor in London. A regular contributor to The Athenaeum, 1858–1901, he wrote several novels, gossipy books on novels and novelists, doctors, lawyers, clergy, etc. Called to the bar at Lincoln's Inn in 1859, he collaborated with William Pole in a life of Robert Stephenson, 1864; became inspector of documents for the Historical Manuscripts Commission, 1874; and wrote *The Real Lord Byron* (1883), *The Real Shelley* (1885), *Lady Hamilton and Lord Nelson* (1888), and *The Queen of Naples and Lord Nelson* (1889). He edited four volumes of the Middlesex County Records, 1886–92, and was author of *A Book of Recollections* (1894).

The Ancient House, Ipswich
in the 1880s

Cutting the branch line to Felixstowe

Suffolk in early and mid-Victorian times must have been very beautiful in its landscapes, much indeed as Constable knew it. There were a number of local artists then practising, who formed a Suffolk School, much on the lines of the Norwich School, followers of Constable. Such for instance was Thomas Churchyard, 1798–1865, born at Woodbridge. He came of farming stock, and was articled to Crabbe and Cross (two good names to be in partnership) of Halesworth, solicitors. He painted Woodbridge and its environs and ranks as one of the finest painters in the Constable circle. He was a friend of FitzGerald, George Crabbe and Bernard Barton.

Robert Burrows, 1810–83, was brother to Sir John noticed above. He was born at Ipswich and, after serving several years in the family business of a pawnbroker, he became a full-time painter and was much influenced by the Norwich School. His early work has been described as mellow, finished and carrying an atmosphere. His skies were pleasantly luminous. His pictures were much sought after even in his lifetime. About 1874 Burrows became very interested in photography and a volume of his work in that field is preserved in the Ipswich library. These are amongst the earliest photographic records of the town.

Henry Bright, 1810–83, was born at Saxmundham, but early moved to Norwich where he came under the influence of that School. He moved to London in 1846, and his income was then stated as around £2,000 a year, which was a lot of money in those days. He sometimes introduces his 'electric' blue pigment into his pictures.

Edward Robert Smythe, 1810–99, was another. Born at Ipswich he ranks as one of the most eminent painters of the Ipswich Group. He became interested in the Norwich School, and is said to have worked with John Sell Cotman. As a draughtsman he ranks high in the Suffolk School, and was extremely fond of horse fairs.

John Duval, 1816–92, moved to Ipswich from Kent in 1852. He was responsible for the illustrations in the first Suffolk *Stud Book*. His chief Suffolk painting was the "Horse Fair in Christchurch Park, 1869". The principal figures in this are all local worthies.

John Moore, 1820–1902, was born at Woodbridge. His father was probably a master plumber, painter and decorator. About

5

1850 he moved to Ipswich. He painted seascapes and local scenes.

Thomas Smythe, 1825–1906, was brother to Edward. He was also born at Ipswich, where he painted his finest pictures. He was known as a landscape and animal painter. He must have been a very kind man because he was described by one of his grand-children as "a dear". He caught the spirit of country life in his day, in pictures such as the "Cottage Door" and "Going to Market".

Henry George Todd, 1846–98, was born at Bury St Edmunds. He later moved to Ipswich. He was a still-life painter, and also produced a fair number of landscapes of Ipswich and the sur-roundings. J. Sheppard, a pupil of John Moore, painted scenes in and around Ipswich, and exhibited 1879–99. George Thomas Rope, 1846–1929, was born at Blaxhall of the farming and barge-owning family. He became an animal painter and his pictures of horses are very fine. He was very local in his work.

(I am indebted for much of this information to those three fine volumes, *East Anglian Painters* by Harold A. E. Day.)

Thomas Woolner, 1825–92, was born at Hadleigh. He was a sculptor and poet. A pupil of Behnes he studied at the Royal Academy in 1842. He made the acquaintance of Rossetti and became one of the original Pre-Raphaelite Brethren in 1847, contributing poems to the *Germ*, but met with but small success in his work. He emigrated to the Australian goldfields in 1852, and his departure inspired Ford Madox Brown's "The Last of England". He returned in 1854.

And some there were who never made the course, such as this, culled from the memorials in St Matthew's Church, Ipswich:

In Memory of
Jabez Hare
who died Feby. 28th., 1837, Aged 17 Yrs.
This tablet is erected by the
subscription of his affectionate friends
as a record of early talent and worth.

(The register reads: "Jabez son of Jabez and Elizabeth Lemon Hare, buried March 6." And the *Ipswich Journal* furnishes the additional particulars that he was a youth of very promising talents as a portrait and animal painter. His likeness in bas-relief appears over the tablet, together with a palette and brushes.)

There were others who came into the county painting Suffolk scenes, such for instance as Frederick William Watts, 1800–1870, of whose career very little is known. His work was so close to Constable's that it was long considered that he had some artistic connection with the Master. But it was later learnt from his widow that he had not received any tuition from Constable. In 1820 Constable was already settled at Hampstead, and from there the next year Watts sent his first contribution to the Royal Academy, the first of seventy-six paintings exhibited there— which with 108 at the British Institution and sixty-five at Suffolk Street, composed the exhibited lifework of one of the best and least known of our minor painters.

Watts remained ten years in Hampstead, only changing to Camden Town in 1831, and to Haverstock Hill seven years later, to remain there for the last thirty-two years of his life. For many years therefore he was Constable's neighbour, and most certainly attended the great man's lectures at the Assembly Rooms in June of 1833 and July of 1836. Watts was a peripatetic painter, but he came into Suffolk and produced some exquisite pictures, some of which have been taken for the work of the Master.

Edward Charles Williams, 1807–81, was another. He was the eldest of Edward Williams' six sons. He is perhaps the best known of Old Williams' children, as in the early part of his artistic career he was very much influenced by the style of the Dutch artists Rysdael, Hobbema and others. In his best Norwich period his paintings were equal to the famous Norwich Master of that time, James Start, and in fact many of his works are wrongly attributed. He travelled throughout the South Country painting meadow-land and village scenes, often painting in refined ochre or pretty rose tints. Some of his Suffolk pictures are very fine.

(I am indebted for this information to Messrs Oscar and Peter Johnson of Lowndes Lodge Gallery, which specializes in views of East Anglia.)

CHAPTER V

A SUFFOLK LINE

———————————••✥••———————————

> For when thou art angry all our days are gone; we bring our years
> to an end as a tale that is told.

My mother's lineage is soon tabled, but it remains an interesting
record of village life as it had been for generations, and as it
remained for much of the Victorian era. It was purely local,
bride and bridegroom coming from the same village, or adjacent
villages—in any case not far apart. The banns were called at the
church and they were married there, walking to the ceremony,
as their fathers before them. It also suggests a close kinship, with
everyone knowing and being related in some way to each other.
In my mother's case, she was of the first generation to leave home
and start a new life amid alien surroundings, carrying the love of
her native countryside in her heart. But it was a way of no return.

I must confess I wonder often how she could have made the
brave venture, accompanied as she was by her black, shiny
covered box. It had been prepared specially for the occasion by
the local wheelwright who was also the undertaker. It was made
like a coffin and decorated with round-headed coffin nails. For
long enough it was by my bedside holding my clothes and few
possessions, and finally it was destroyed by bombs in World
War II.

But how did she get it across London from Bishopsgate
station? Surely those bearded porters, who probably spoke her
language, must have treated her with the kindness of which they
were so capable.

The line begins at Middleton-cum-Fordley, with a (1) Samuel
Barham who married a Rachel Bickers, both of the parish, in
1799. They made their home at a little lath and plaster cottage,
known as The Pantiles. It was adjacent to an old farm at the bend

of a once very dangerous bit of road that runs past manor house to the Yew Tree corner. In Samuel's time it was an ideal spot for the smuggling which must have been rife in his day, set as it was in a particularly lovely bit of old Suffolk, low lying in the mists of time. Even now the garden outline can still be traced by certain fruit trees that Samuel may have planted. Alas, poor Rachael died in 1802.

On the 12th October 1804 Samuel married again, this time a Mary Woolnough, also of the parish. David Packard was the curate and John Bedwell the parish clerk. They had issue eight children, and as a family populated the village during the Victorian era. There were (2) Henry, 1806; (3) Samuel 1808, died an infant; (4) Sophia, 1809; (5) Samuel, 1812; (6), Elizabeth 1814; (7) John, 1817; (8) Naomi, 1819; (9) Francis, 1822.

It is perhaps interesting to note that of the 198 marriages recorded in the registers from 1754 to 1804, some of which were re-marriages, no less than 105 of the bridegrooms were unable to write; and whereas in some cases the men could, the women couldn't. Further, the curious fact comes to light that Samuel Barham, Rachael Bickers and Samuel Strange, the witness, all signed by their marks. But when Samuel re-married he wrote his name quite clearly—"Sam. Barham"—whereas Mary Woolnough and Henry Watling the witness used marks. One wonders how Samuel came to write; it seems to suggest willingness and ability to learn. He was buried on 15th August, aged 48, so that Francis would have been a posthumous child. His wife lived on until December 1857, dying at the age of 77.

Pursuing the line down, (2) Henry married Mary Baggett, 1827, and had issue; (10) Henry, 1827; (11) John, 1829; (12) James, 1831, died 1846.

Now comes (5) Samuel Barham, married to Sippa [sic] Smith of the parish of Aldboro, 1834. He must have been the member of that family who went into the service of the irascible and litigious Newson Garrett of Snape and Aldeburgh fame; and is so delightfully described in *What I Remember* by Millicent Fawcett, the wife of the blind Postmaster General.

Number 7 is another John, who married a Mahala Brown in 1840. She was my grandmother's elder sister, and by marrying John she also became her aunt. He was known as 'Gardener'

Barham. Although he died in 1873 and Mahala in 1889, they have the distinction of a double mourning card, complete with a wide black border. So it must have been printed after the death of Mahala. These cards were an essential feature of the protocol of mourning, and were often brought out and conned over after the Christmas feast. A more appropriate occasion would have been All Souls' Day.

They had issue: (13) Joseph, (14) Joshua and (15) John. Joseph married Rhoda Broom, daughter of the first Middleton post-master, who carried on after her father's death. They had issue: (16) Herbert, who remained unmarried; and (17) Milton, who became a solicitor at Woodbridge. He had issue two sons.

We now go back to: (9) Francis Barham, described as of the parish of Westleton, who married Clara Crisp, December 1845. They had issue: (18) Jonah, (19) Robert and (20) Thomas.

Jonah in turn married Susan Pulham and had issue: (21) Samuel, who was succeeded by (22) Aubrey.

Number 10 is Henry, son of the first Henry. He married Rebecca Butcher at the beginning of 1850 with no issue. I have dealt with this delightful old pair in a later chapter.

This brings me to (11) John, brother to Henry, married to Susannah Brown at the end of 1850 or beginning of 1851. Their firstborn was my mother, Eliza. Then came (23) Allen, after whom I was named. He was buried 13th January 1869, aged 9. His early death was an abiding sorrow to my grandmother. Next came (24) Charles, who married Hannah Stollery of Westleton, and had three daughters but no son. Two more girls completed grandfather's quiver: Rebecca, who never married, and through the turmoil of the Second World War lies in Middleton churchyard; and Susannah, likewise, who is buried at Hingham, Norfolk.

An entry in the first *Stud Book* can be linked up with the marriage of (18) Jonah, above, with Susan Pulham. It reads: "Samuel Pulham was born in 1792; he lives at Middleton, and but for times' mark on his hair might pass for a man of sixty-five. In this year of grace 1879, he hoes mangold, stirs as quick, and speaks as sharp as most men of just half his age. . . . To Sam Pulham and his neighbour old John Bloomfield, of Leiston, I wish to extress my grateful thanks; they took the trouble to meet me and help to unravel histories (of Suffolk Punches), of which they knew the inns-and-outs, and no one else. Poor old John, whose habits had become a little irregular, has of late consigned himself to the care of the master of Bulcamp House of Industry."

Samuel Pulham was a contemporary of my great, great grandfather, and at one time lived at the manor house, still standing with its outbuildings, where my grandfather died. He and his wife kept cows, and one of them managed to get poor old Grandmother Pulham down and kicked her in the chest. This resulted in a cancer from which she died. Samuel was classed as a groom, and one of Jonah's daughters (born 1888), still alive, told me he was a rare man for horses.

The old church registers in which so many of these names appear contain a number of extremely interesting notes. For example this: "Robert Edgar Wood, Middleton, 23 July, 1886, 4 weeks. This child was found dead in bed, and not having been baptised, the Rev. J. A. Clowes (Vicar of Westleton), performed an appropriate service in the church porch."

Neither can I leave out the entry concerning Moses, Miriam and Aaron, triplets born to Hannah and John Chapman, labourer, on 1st June 1839 and baptized on the third of the same month. Whether they survived their entry into a fallen world I cannot say. Before them, long before, had been a Barzillai and Tabitha Ayton, brother and sister. And the Aytons had also produced an Adam and Eve, who died as infants.

There are no complications of this family tree of not too many branches, but it is pure Suffolk. In many ways it is a simple Christian's idea of heaven, for in most part our picture of the heavenly state does not go much further back than two or three generations.

> Go! loved one, to the bosom of thy mother,
> Meet there the smile in infancy thine own.
> Meet there thy infant brother,
> Knowing in heaven, whom thou on earth hast known.

The mind boggles after that, and we are left to deal with the countless host of strangers. These names of yesteryear are, one and all, of the soil—owned in part by Lord Huntingfield, but which he had to leave *in situ* when he passed over.

CHAPTER VI

THE OLD GREAT EASTERN

···⟨⟩···

In memory of Owen Owen, Engine Driver, who died 5th April 1872, aged 29:

> His last drive is over, death has put on the brake,
> His soul has been signalled its last journey to take,
> When death sounds its whistle, the steam of life falls,
> And his mortal clay shunted till the last trumpet calls.

Railway fever was a disease that broke out in the early years of Queen Victoria, and, like the common cold, it has never been conquered. Every now and again a fresh epidemic breaks out, the chief symptoms being twinges of memory, nostalgic nausea and steaming perspiration. It even causes people to call out as in a trance.

I was born so near a railway station that I almost feel to be of that pedigree, neither can I ever forget my first remembered journey into the delectable land of my mother's birthplace—Suffolk. Indeed, I am so old that I can remember the time when lamps were let into the top of the carriages by men operating on the roof, one per carriage; also there were those enormous old metal containers holding hot water that could be hired for a shilling and made a journey on a biting cold day at least bearable. Then there were those immense wooden gantries holding aloft the semaphore signals. At our local station a porter used to carry a paper flambeau and knock it into life as he climbed the ladder to light the signal lamps. The gas lamps on the station were turned low in between times, and up when the train was coming; while oil lamps on the country stations are within recent memory. Neither can I forget the eeriness of the Ipswich tunnel, or the pleasant-looking man with his long-handled hammer who tapped the wheels—although I feel sure he didn't stop long enough to hear if they were cracked.

Third Class 1837

An open box—a cattle truck,
Exposed to wind, and rain, and muck,
The flap-door falls—a racking plane
Up which you run your track to gain;
Within, you stand, a herd of swine—
This on a first-class London Line.

Third Class 1899

A carpet floor—a cushion'd seat—
A toilet service—all complete;
A sixty-mile an hour feed—
A table d'hote in spite of speed;
A chair in which to sleep or smoke;
All things to ease the travelling joke;
The panorama rushes by—
A picture pleasing to the eye;
The woods, the streams, the fields, the hills,
Announcing every kind of pills;
You read them all and cannot tell
The pill that's best to keep you well;
So go to sleep before you're flustered,
And dream you're taking "Beecham's Mustard."

Punch

The old Great Eastern line has had a very interesting history. It was mooted as long ago as 1824 as the Norfolk, Suffolk and Essex Railroad. This finally took shape in 1836 as the Eastern Counties Railway, with permission to construct a railway from London to Yarmouth via Chelmsford, Colchester and Ipswich, starting from Devonshire Street, Shoreditch. When it reached Chelmsford the capital of the company ran out, but new money was subscribed to finish the line to Colchester in 1843. The company then applied successfully to be relieved of the remainder of their statutory obligations. Ipswich soon took advantage of this, and, by leaving the town at 7 a.m. by the 'Quicksilver Coach' and changing to the train at Colchester, it became possible to spend five hours in London and return to Ipswich by the same method in a day.

It looked very much as though Ipswich would be deprived of a railway communication with London. Led by Mr John Chevallier Cobbold, however, a sum of £200,000 was raised and the Eastern Union Railway was formed. An Act was obtained in July 1844 and the construction of the line was commenced to connect to the Eastern Counties line at Colchester. This section was planned by Peter Bruff. (See also No. 49, Class 7, Great Exhibition catalogue.)

A deep cutting had to be made at Brantham, and the Stour was crossed by two viaducts on piles. A temporary station at Ipswich was built on the southern outskirts of the town, near Croft Street, Stoke, in a position to take the line round Stoke Hill if desired, by an embankment to a more centrally placed station near the present cattle market. This, however, was not carried out, owing mainly to shortage of material to form the embankment, and a curve was consequently thrown off to the left before the temporary Stoke station was reached, as an approach to the tunnel to be cut under the hill.

The Eastern Union Railway, a 5-feet gauge line, was first used for goods traffic on 1st June 1846, but on 11th June, the formal opening ceremony took place, when a train drawn by two engines left Ipswich for Colchester at 10.30 a.m. to meet a train from London arriving there at 11.45. Both trains carried the directors, engineers and supporters of the two companies, and after coupling the twenty carriages together they returned to Ipswich at 1.30 p.m. After being received with all sorts of joyfulness, with ringing of bells and with guns firing, the company walked through the grounds of Mr C. F. Gower (now occupied by Waterside Works) to the riverside, and after a most excellent lunch a trip was made to Harwich and back by the *River Queen*.

The rest of the day was spent in celebrating the occasion by the officers, the contractors and townsfolk. The day concluded with a balloon ascent, and after dark a display of fireworks, the special return train arriving at Shoreditch at 1 a.m.

The rolling stock of the Eastern Union Railway consisted of eight locomotives, first, second and third-class carriages, luggage and freight trucks, the offices being situated in Brook Street. The line, after being inspected, was opened for passenger traffic on 15th June 1846.

Work was proceeding with the tunnel under Stoke Hill, and rapid progress was being made with the construction of the Ipswich and Bury Company's line through Needham Market and Stowmarket to Bury. This line is 26½ miles long, and as there was no engineering works of any importance the opening ceremony took place on 7th December 1846. A special train bringing directors and friends was run from Shoreditch, and after picking up guests at Ipswich the journey was continued through scenes of much rejoicing towards Bury. Stations, bridges etc, were gaily decorated, and at Stowmarket a group of 'labourers' copiously toasted the directors and friends from half a cask of beer. The Northgate Station was described as an extensive pile of buildings in the Elizabethan style erected in 1847 from designs by Mr Sancton Wood.

On 24th December the line was opened for passenger traffic, but, as the Ipswich station on the north side of the tunnel was not ready, up trains were passed through the tunnel and backed into the temporary station at Croft Street, which was single sided. The up platform of the present passenger station was not in use until 1860, and this was followed by the down, or island platform in 1883. It might also be mentioned that the terminus at Liverpool Street was completed in 1875.

A timetable used in 1848 shows that four trains down and four up were scheduled, the first leaving Bury at 6 a.m., Ipswich at 7 a.m. and arriving in London at 10.5 a.m.; and the last train down leaving London at 4.45 p.m., reaching Ipswich 8.5, and arriving at Bury 9.19. First, second and third–class carriages were available on most trains. The fares from Ipswich to London were: first class 14s. 6d., second 11s., third 7s. 6d.; and Parliamentary 5s. 7½d. (a train both ways, at least once a day at a penny a mile).

The works were originally at Romford, but later removed to Stratford, where a Mr John Gooch built the first engine in 1850, a 2-2-2 well-tank engine, with outside cylinders. The Eastern Union had their works at Ipswich, but they were very small. On amalgamation they were transferred to Stratford. There was a plan to remove them from there to Bury in the 1880s.

I discovered the following in a volume of the monumental inscriptions of St Matthew's, Ipswich, dated 1884.

Samuel Davys Bowman
assistant engineer
on the
Eastern Union
and
Ipswich & Bury Railways
died April 11, 1846
aged 23 years.
Regretted by all who knew his worth.
His friend Peter Bruff,
who held him in deserved
estimation erected
this Monument to his
memory.

Was it not rather young to be an engineer at 23?

Verity Anderson in her book *The Northrepps Grandchildren*, gives a very excellent account of the cutting of new lines:

It was a great event when the railway reached Cromer in 1877, thus ending the coaching days. It had been brought gradually nearer, and as a preliminary, the navvies mapped out the line by digging away the soil and then leaving it for some months. When the summer came, millions of field poppies appeared and the scarlet ribbon stretching for miles was a most remarkable and lovely sight. At last came the time when the line was finished and the first train of three heavy engines and their tenders tried the rails and bridges bit by bit, to the astonishment of the villagers and cattle.

It was all part of a network that had been spread over north Norfolk. With those small flint built booking offices and paraffin-lit waiting rooms with fires burning in their cottage-type grates, their stations were sleepy places except in the summer season when the trippers passed through them, and on market days, when sheep and cattle and farm produce left the goods yards.

She also recounts joining the train at Stratford station: "Soon the train came up, and it was the greatest interest to us all getting into the saloon carriage. It certainly was most comfortable and beautifully fitted up. There was a table in the middle, two nice easy chairs, a sofa fixed to the wall at one side, and two seats at the other, there was also a little carriage opening into the big one, which we called the nursery and there was a wash-hand basin with plenty of beautiful water. Then there was a Second Class carriage attached to the First Class, also a place for luggage."

In 1826 a project to build a line from Ipswich to Eye was raised, but while it is believed it was intended to use horses for traction, the railway never developed.

The line from Haughley through Diss to Norwich was constructed and opened in sections, with an official opening in Norwich on 7th November 1849 at Victoria Station. A line had previously been in use from Yarmouth to Norwich since 1st May 1844, and an extension was opened to Brandon and Cambridge on 30th July 1845. In consequence the principal towns in East Anglia were now in direct railway communication.

A branch line to Hadleigh from Bentley was opened on 21st August 1847, and an Act of 9th July 1847, enabled the Ipswich and Bury line to be extended to Woodbridge. The line was ultimately carried to Beccles.

An extension from Bury to Norwich was built in 1849 and another to Newmarket in 1854. This latter produced the wonderful station that is now causing a problem to the railway authorities. It is described as a unique example of the early Victorian period, baroque in style with Ionic pillars. It gives the appearance of an orangery of a stately house. It was built mainly to take the race-horse traffic for the Newmarket meetings.

In 1862 the various railway companies operating in or near Ipswich were amalgamated to form the Great Eastern Railway. This old line was blessed by several good chairmen, such as Lord Salisbury, who was followed by Mr Parkes, who gave his name to Parkeston Quay. Then in 1893 came Lord Claud Hamilton, after whom the famous class of engines was named.

The Mid-Suffolk Light Railway was incorporated in October 1900. This ran from Haughley to Laxfield, via Mendlesham, Aspall, Kenton, Horham and Stradbroke—in other words through the very heart of Suffolk—and was an attempt at filling up a gap in the railway map. Light railways were being planned in large numbers after an 1896 Act of Parliament, and the Mid-Suffolk was one of these.

The Felixstowe branch line, which ran from Westerfield, began life privately owned, having been built by Colonel Tomline on his own land. The project was set on foot as early as the '60s, but did not materialize until 1877, when it was opened for traffic.

In those early days there were two station masters at Westerfield: William Charles Harrison for the G.E.R. and Arthur Flower for the Felixstowe railway. This may account for the rather commodius, double-sided booking office, now standing forlornly destitute. It appears it was to have been part of a larger enterprise to include a Felixstowe, Ipswich and Midlands Company 1886, but never came to anything. Colonel Tomline sold his venture in 1887 to the Great Eastern, who, it appears, had worked it since 1879.

When the new line was built an inspector from the Board of Trade walked ahead of an engine from Westerfield to the Beach Station, inspecting the track, the stations and sidings. A Mr Read, who afterwards became station master at the Beach Station accompanied him from Westerfield, of which station he was station master. This was a most picturesque affair which the Colonel had built for himself amongst the Seven Hills of Nacton and was named Orwell Park. There was no station at Trimley.

The following day there was an official opening of the railway, and the Colonel was the first person to book a ticket. Mr Read personally handed him one numbered 0001, for a first-class return journey from Orwell to the Beach. Read went to the Beach Station in 1882 and remained there until 1898, when he was transferred to the Town Station, where he remained until 1920, retiring then after fifty-two years' service.

Colonel Tomline ran the line himself for a short time and dressed the staff in the mode of his household servants. For example, the guard was uniformed as a butler, and one of the first picturesque copper-nob engines was named "The Tomline". The railway was under the management of a Mr Kirtley and the traffic steadily increased until at length the Great Eastern Railway was ready to buy. It was said that the Colonel was never reconciled to parting with his favourite enterprise, for he regarded the bigger railway as an unclean beast. Five branch lines were built in connection with the Ipswich–Beccles line, and this Felixstowe branch is the only one that remains.

There is a good deal of picturesque record of the early days of the line, including one of actually digging the track (facing page 65). The equipment then deemed necessary consisted of picks and shovels, and a pair of uncommonly strong arms. Not yet had the patent excavator for railways and canals as invented and shown at the Great Exhibition by Ransomes and May been adopted. But you will not fail to notice the fine array of country headgear then in use. No two heads appear to be alike. The trace-horse is of interest because these fine old animals were much used for shunting and knew their job. They were particularly noticeable at Woodbridge. When the photograph was taken these men were called navvies, derived from navigator; and that is really what they are doing.

The original route ran to the Beach Station, and when visitors came they went to this station and then to get to the town took a horsed cab, which cost a shilling. Even in those early days the railway company ran trips to London for 5s. return. A correspondent informed me that his parents often laughed at the posters which read: "Day Excursion to London, Non-Stop (stopping at Trimley only), fare 5/ return."

On 1st July 1898, a short spur was opened to the Town Station, and this is what the railway booklet had to say about it: "Mr John Wilson, the chief engineer, has built the station in a style which harmonises with its aristocratic surroundings." It goes on to note: ". . . the unique appearance of the long platform, 25 ft. wide, which is covered for 500 ft. with a lantern roof, supported with light iron columns carrying graceful arches. The effect is very pleasing." Alas, this great advance for the town is coming to an end and will soon disappear.

As with all others in those days of individuality, some of the porters were great characters. For example the one at Saxmundham when asked by a nervous passenger if this was the train for Aldeburgh, replied, "Git yow in thare together". She looked round for the others but found she was alone. Or the porter at Wickham Market who forgot his lines: "Change here for Marlesford, Parham and Franningham-Wickham Market! All change here, some on yer!"

Another line was planned from Westerfield but came to nothing. The account reads:

The Duke of Cambridge, who never grows old, travelled all the way to Westerfield, to cut the first sod of the new light railway on Saturday last (May, 1902); and there need be no hesitation in saying that the scheme to which he lent his countenance is distinctly worthy. It will open direct communication from Cambridge and the adjacent parts of the Midlands to the East Coast; it will also provide communication for a whole series of market towns and villages which have been forced hitherto to rely upon the roads. In fact such a railway has long been the dream of East Anglia; and it is a good omen that its directors and promoters are, in the main, local gentlemen who have a stake in the county. The gauge is 4 ft. 8½ ins, so that it will carry Great Eastern rolling stock. In fact all things promise well for it, and the Great Eastern, for its own sake, will, no doubt, give every encouragement to the new enterprise.

Needless to say, jokes ran about these small railways, such as the one about a farmer who bought a 'hin' house at a Suffolk Show. A few weeks later he had a postcard to say that it was at the Mid-Suffolk station awaiting collection.

One morning he said to his carter Ephraim, "Eff, put Diamond in the tumbrel and go down to the station an' git thet owd hin house I bought at the Show, will yer."

So Eff went as directed, and when he got back he drove into the yard and said to the master, "Hare's yar hin house."

The farmer looked at it and exclaimed, "Hin house be damned, thass the ticket orfice!"

But how fine it was in that great age of steam to sit on a bit of rising ground and watch the plume of smoke threading a way through the countryside—there was so much of it with the great coal trade that was built up in Ipswich. The milk trains with their jingle and rattle of cans being loaded into or out of the vans. And there would be the hurrying whistle of the fish train as it made its way over the pile bridges with its perishable load. It was all taken for granted. One could hear the sounds as one lay comfortably in bed, with sometimes a hollowness. One could never foresee that a time would come when it would end.

> O My agèd Uncle Arly!
> Sitting on a heap of Barley
>   Thro' the silent hours of night,—
> Close beside a leafy thicket:—
> On his nose there was a Cricket,—
>   In his hat a Railway-Ticket;—
> (But his shoes were far too tight.)
>   Edward Lear

Beach Station, Felixstowe

Three Dennington celebrities, whose combined age was 265

Polly Vincent

Uncle Harry and Great Aunt Rebecca

CHAPTER VII

COUNTRY SCENES AND CHARACTERS

——————··✠··——————

1. POLLY VINCENT

It is a long time now since I watched her muddling about in her little kitchen and listened to the constant murmur of despair and despondency that came from her lips. Yet I can remember her so well, her flickering eyelids, the roundness of her face, her grubby hands; even the one or two hairs that grew on her upper lip. I can recall her old boots that shuffled about the brick floor and her everlasting head-dress and bedraggled garments, that unlike the ocean never saw a change.

There was no incandescent blue light of television in those days, or a constancy of suave words announcing this and that; yet she was not lonely. She had her old cat that looked at one with a surly sort of face as though it had been brought up in a work-house. And there was the pig just round the corner that greeted her with a certain familiarity if she should go anywhere near it. In some strange way they were all related, Suffolk through and through, with hands and feet deep set in a distant past. Sufficient for her that Napoleon was dead (at least she had 'heerd' her mother say he was) and that the son of a Suffolk mother had given him a rare good rousting. Besides, her father had been one of the ringers for the funeral of poor old Silly Billy, alias William IV when he was buried. But, thare she must git the wittals ready time poor brother Tom and poor brother Fred should come home from their respective labours. Her old clock seemed to fairly race round, even running into tomorrow.

How she came to be grandmother's 'nabor' I wouldn't know. She must have come from somewhere, out of the everywhere that was the village, into just there, but as a little boy I didn't enquire into those things. Neither, for that matter, had grand-mother and grandfather always lived at Rackford farm, although in my childish ignorance I thought they had. It was certain they weren't there when my mother was born, and that was a long way back before my time. No, Polly must have moved in at some Michaelmas or the other when poor dear Tom and Fred decided to make a change in location but not in occupation. All the same, it was from somewhere in the parish of Middleton-cum-Fordley. Where else could it have been? That was her native and her life would have been shortened if she had had to leave it. She knew every cabbage in her bit of garden and every leaf on every cabbage. Did not father and mother peer out from some of those old casements, that had let in the light between the pot plants since Elizabeth, our Queen and Governor, had taken what she could of her subjects (her dogs who wore her collars) and given nothing in return? And were not those parents lying there somewhere near the linden tree in that little square acre that must have been several corpses deep, under the shadow of that rubble-walled steeple? But that was time of parson Packard, who wore a wig.

I don't know if Polly ever went out to church or to chapel, but surely she must have gone to Broom's shop for a little mite o' this, or a pennorth o' that. Come to think on't, she had known him since he was a little owd bor, a regular run-about he was. Her old father used to say he'd skin a raisin lest he gave one too many come Christmas. Howsomever, she had a great regard for Mr White, the rector. He was a gentleman if you like. Some said he had travelled as far away as India. She couldn't bear to think of them horrible heathens, some with no legs, fingers or a nose; or people with their eyes and mouth in the wrong places. Fancy living along o' them. Suppose one should come to her backhouse door, talking in one o' them foreign tongues, so that you couldn't tell whether he wur using bad language, or merely asking for a crust of bread. She would have shruck out if one did come. But there, Mr White knew a thing or two about medicine, even more than Liz. Button who could cure burns. He did right well with Kezia Hunt when she fell ill with the palsey (or suffen). He give her some stuff that hiked her out of bed some quick, although uncharitable folks said that worn't nawthin' but a bit of old bindweed that some folks called jalap. Then he had the cheek to say he hooped he'd see her at the eight o'clock sarvice, when he'd give her sixpence out of the collection plate. Ah, some nice gentleman he were, driving about in his carriage with a Barham coachman, wearing a cock's comb of a thing, like the squire's man. And didn't he keep that new rectory nice he had had built, them paths were sanded every Saturday as regular as clockwork.

There is one thing very certain, that, inquisitive as I was, I never penetrated the interior of Polly's cottage home farther than the backhouse. You may think it was a smelly place, but that was not so, there was a country flavour that pervaded all such home-steads and such people. There would be a fire smouldering in the grate, more of wood than of any other fuel, although coal came to them via the billiboy ketches and old Dunwich. A fire to me was always a pleasant thing at any time of the year, and after all, it was not always that hot in April when the cowslips blew, which my mother so much loved and when we visited her home.

Polly would not have been able to read or write and by that unencumberance she was relieved of a lot of worry and burden. As she had no neighbours she could not gossip, neither did she suffer from any anguish that might have been hers in the race for possessions that neither filled the belly nor calmed the mind. Her mother had left her a few bits of earthenware needed in domestic life, and above all her old brewing and baking things. What more could anyone want, save perhaps a good feather bed. No, she had no 'larnin' ', she left that to the parson. After all, he didn't seem all that satisfied with his attainments, as he was always scrabbin' after more books and more of this, that and the tother, to make life that much the fuller. If I had managed to get into her pantry even, I might have seen a little bit or two of blue pottery, like as not "A Present from Lowestoft".

From the foregoing you might conclude that Polly was ignorant, but I do not think so. She knew a great deal about elementary things, which we have lost in the wild overgrowth of modern learning and living. A lonely life such as was hers was a wonderful preservative of originality and purity of breed. She hardly had need of a clock, because her two great timepieces were the sun and the moon; the latter, if anything of far greater importance than the former, because it ruled the weather. I wonder what would have been her reaction if she could have

known that years after she was dead and lying near her people,
that men had actually climbed up to the moon. "Lawks a mussy,"
she might have exclaimed, she knew there was one ther "a-riddy",
for she had seen him. At night, oh so dark, she would have
known something of the stars, but she was away in sleep too soon
to be troubled by them. She lived in the past, and yet she didn't,
because the old ways were her ways, and the future held nothing
better. The signs of the zodiac did not change.

Her knowledge of the parish was complete, she knew who lived
at the various homesteads and who had lived there, where there
was the likelihood of meeting a ghost, or the black dog Shuck.

You must realize that in those days almost every house of any
size had a ghost in one of its rambling rooms. People were gifted
with second sight and had presentiments; and it is a curious fact
that these visitations never troubled cottages, they favoured the
more spacious apartments of the large old manor houses. As two
of the servants were alleged to have said at one of the nearby
halls: "If you please ma'am, Mrs Rous and me must change our
room. We can't nohow remain where we are, ma'am: thass
sartin'. The ghost, he make sich a noise ooover our hids, we can't
git no sleep at all."

Here then, by way of digression is a true story about a house
that was haunted by a man who was accused of having built it
with tainted money. It was told by a Suffolk native to his vicar.

No, sir, I don't believe as how he walk now; tain't likely. But then
yew know he ded, sir, time past. They du sah one time there allus
used to be a knife and fork laid out for he ivery night, but at last they
couldn't stand it no longer, and they got the passon in, an' he read he
down in a closet agin the fireplace in the best bedroom an' they
papered the closet door up, an' he wornt heard no more iver so long.
Then there come some new people, an' took the house, an' they
undone the closet; an' aout he come rasher nor iver, knocken'
here an' knocken' thare, tell yow couldn't hardly sleep for he. An'
that I know for a trewth, cos my mother's brother's wife's father,
he was a wheelwright, heerd him agin an' agin, an' so he told me
hisself. Then they read him daoun agin. That time they read he
down of a clock case, an' they took the pendle aout, an' put it
down of a well. So he wor squat of a long time; but arterwards they
got the pendle agin, an' set the clock agoin', an' aout he come
rasher nor iver, knockin' an' carryin' on that they couldn't abear

themselves. So that time they got a hape o' passons to read he down for good. I don't know zackly haow many there was, there was tharty passons [probably churchwardens, parish clerks and sextons were included in the number] comed together from all raound, an' they read he daown of an oud well, an' they built a summer-haouse over it in what they call the Park; an' that haven't been interfered with sence. So taint likely he don't walk now: yow don't think so yourself, sir, now du ye?

Polly took good care that she kept indoors when the old Jack-o-lanterns were about. But then, poor brother Tom suffered from moon madness, and there was no knowing what he might do. But, as I have said, her knowledge of the parish was vast, considering she lived so lonely a life. She knew who was the baldest man in the village—some old gipsy had huffed his hair off—and who was the hairiest; and how many teeth old Mother Lumkin had in her head. By the time I knew her she was nearly as good as the church registers for births, marriages and deaths.

But there was one occasion in her life when she was whooly scared. She was out right late (probably not later than nine o'clock). It was a dark night and she felt she was being followed, regular pursued. She felt a cold shiver go down her back, an' heerd footsteps behind her. The faster she walked the faster the owd thing came on until she paked over her shoulders when she saw a horrid shape a coming along as though on its hind legs. When she eventually gained home she gazed out from her little window, and would you believe it, that was an owd dickey without a head, as trew as I'm a telling on yew, together.

I think Polly's religious sympathies were with the chapel folk, certainly poor brother Fred's were. He used to scrape a way up the stairs to the little gallery, lean on the ledge and look down on the fustian coated congregation. (I wonder if that gallery still finds a few sitters in.) Because you must know church folk were a bit on the establishment side. They were perfectly certain they had the Petrine keys in their keeping.

If anyone fell ill she predicted in her own mind a sudden end, but she much preferred a lingering death. It was not without significance that the churchyard was in the centre of the village, because the dead were not dead. Then, of course, it was to be the scene of the Resurrection. (Augustus Hare once remarked:

"What a grand sight it will be when twelve Dukes of Hamilton rise together.") All the same, Polly shuddered when she heard the passing bell giving out its mournful record of years.

That brings to mind that, although life was so peaceful and quiet, the air was heavy with certain sounds. Polly all her life had listened to the church bells, because it was a pleasantly vibrant steeple, sometimes entering into great events that touched the parish but little, or calling folks to arly sarvice and that of the mid-morning.

> To the True God, my *tongue* gives Laud;
>   My chimes the Clergy know:
> My clapper loud collects the Crowd;
>   For Death I toll in woe;
> With holy knell no Plague can dwell . . .
>   No Feasts of Saints without Saint Bell.

Then there came the rumbling in the distance of the trains, something her grandfather never knew, because the railway was only built when she was a gal. Another sound was made by the wind soughing in the trees, particularly the trembling aspen by the horse pond that never grew dry. And lastly the sea in the willowy green of the distance, awful at certain times of the year as it thundered on the surf (sometimes they wondered if it would come riding across the meadows), and the wrecks were piled up along the coast. But all these sounds were the creatures of the wind.

I don't suppose I ran any errands for Polly, although I did for my grandmother, in collecting the milk in a little cylindrical tin can with a handle and a lid. It was always such a nice little trip across the fields in the scented air of the morning. Polly must have had some means of getting hers, because it wasn't brought to her backhouse door, nor the butter neither. But the bread was, such lovely bread from Leiston in a little pony cart, covered over with mealy sacks and delivered by a pleasant man who used to tie up his pony at the farmyard gate. Bread meant a great deal for the poor brothers and helped to fill their linen wittal pokes, the contents of which they consumed under the trees of a friendly hedge.

The brothers, by the way, never seemed to be on the same job together. Farm labouring was always a lonely job, working solo, miles away in the hinterland; sometimes they never saw another soul all day. But if they hadn't got a watch they knew when it was time to go home, although they weren't all that careful as to an exact minute. There was no mechanical farming, it was all "spade work and sweat of their brows".

I don't know what sort of an upbringing Polly had had. I suppose she began life in sarvice, and it may be she never progressed beyond scullery maid. Anyhow, she looked upon the gentry and the young ladies as though they had come down to earth from some other planet and their skins were different; besides, the blood in their veins was blue. Then perhaps she got a job in a farmhouse to help with the dairy, but what with the woman always demanding scalding water and the cantankerous old farmer grumbling about her not making an appearance before 4.30 in the morning, she had enough of that and thought she would be better off at Bulcamp. Besides, he was a nasty old man, used to say she lay in bed as though she'd got a man with 'er. "But yew han't hev yew?" he would remark. She had been brought up respectable and wasn't having any of that talk, thank you. Then the old place had a ghost that came clinking upstairs at all sorts of funny hours, and you never knew when you might run up against it. Shortly after both father and mother died and she came home to look after her two brothers, and by such a move achieved a certain amount of independence.

One must recall the times in which she lived, the autocracy of the upper classes, the formalism in religion, the sadistic propensities in dealing with children. That so-called religious God-fearing men could take a horsewhip to their own boys, that girls could be shut up in cupboards and made to do penance for trivial offences. All done as a supposed foundation stone to character, well and truly laid. It is hardly to be wondered that some developed a suspicious and eccentric character. It was a morbid age, with every one taking a deep interest in the business of dying, and when premonitions of death (not life) were to be met with on every hand.

Polly resented anyone poking into her business. She didn't poke into theirs and she certainly was giving no biographical details of her own. I don't suppose even Mrs Sarah Trippitt called with her lidded basket, with bits of napery and trimmings and household wares. She would have known it was of no avail. That is why the photograph (facing page 81) is so wonderful, remembering it was taken before the snapshot came into view. But it has caught her well enough, dressed in the mode of the day, thinking her own thoughts, going about her own affairs. She would have been whooly riled if she had known. But there she is, in her wide, highly fashionable chip-straw hat (how did she come by it? Surely from out of the ladies at Theberton Hall and Bond Street; never from any local bandbox), her shawl, bodice, voluminous skirt over more than one red flannel petticoat; and her white apron and long fingers. It is high summer but she makes no concessions to that. Presumably she has just got a pail of soft water from the butt, the top of which latter is covered over by a bit of sacking to act as a filter. Notice too, the nice old slender prop in the corner with its equally slender shadow, derived from some hedgrow; and the 'grinstooon', that comes into service occasionally for knives, flashing hooks or a scythe blade.

I don't suppose a man, other than her brothers, ever came into her life. She didn't envy any one their lot, and in too many cases she had no need. Her world was her village and she wanted for 'nawthen', since she always drove her own pair (legs); and as long as she could scrab about that was all she asked of life. "Lawk," she would say, "we all have our trooials, an' now I aren't so bad as pore old Job what had to scraaope hisself." But as with all her generation, brought up in a feudal Suffolk, her end came in that First Great War; although she had never acquired the habit of being ill. They hurried her poor old body to lie with all the others, on a day when a bleak wind swept over everywhere so that even the flowers could not sit still. And in sheer desperation poor brother Fred entered into matrimony with a gal in the village.

2. GREAT AUNT REBECCA

Suffolk villages at the time of my grandfather were not altogether self-contained, but their outlying contacts were within walking distance, although that radius might extend as widely as 20 miles. How the male members of the family went a-courting so far afield is difficult to know, since their day's labour was from dawn to dusky eve. Perhaps it came about they hired themselves out to farmers in surrounding villages and there met the one to whom they remained constant for the rest of their time. It must be realized that I entered into this kind of life when I went to Middleton with my mother as a little boy, because the lovely spell had not yet been broken. You may think this was a deadly dull way of life, but I can assure you it was a sight better than life in the built-up areas of London's suburbia, to which so many of their children gravitated. But even then, places like Camberwell, Norwood, Highgate, Highbury and Clapham could offer pretty little areas almost as peaceful.

I think my grandfather married a girl from the village, but his brother Henry went as far afield as Knodishall to find his bride. Although it was a good ten miles away it was in the same hundred, and was very similar to Middleton in character. Here is what William White wrote of it in 1855:

Knodishall, or Knoddishall, has a number of scattered houses and the village of Coldfair Green. It has in its parish 432 souls and 1829 acres of land, including Buxlow, or Buxlee, which was anciently a separate parish, and had a church, the site of which is now in a garden. The manor of Knodishall was for a long period held by the Jenny family, and now belongs to the Rev. G. A. Wilkinson, but part of the soil belongs to Lord Huntingfield, and the Vernon, Girling, Bloomfield, and other families and a small part of the parish is in the manor of Leiston. The Church (St. Lawrence) is an ancient structure, which was thoroughly renovated in 1846. The Rectory of Knodishall, with Buxlow curacy annexed to it, is valued in KB at £11, and now at £486, in the patronage and incumbency of the Rev. G. A. Whittaker, M.A., who has 15 acres of glebe, and a commodious rectory house, built in 1838. At Coldfair Green is a small Primitive Methodist Chapel, erected in 1853.

In those far off days the village held seven farmers, three blacksmiths, three shoemakers—one of which was a Joseph Munnings, surely a good old Suffolk name that was to become famous in the art world of these present years. Then follows a corn miller, butcher, tailor; and the inn was the 'Butcher's Arms', kept by a butcher. It was one of Suffolk's fat livings, if we consider what £486 was worth in those days as compared with these. The vicar must have been a gentleman indeed in the eyes of poor men earning 8s. a week. Did he take fees of them when they came to him to wed or were brought to him at death? I wonder. The parish clerk was William Scarlett. But please note, Lord Huntingfield who owned the soil was not able to take any of it with him when he went to heaven.

Now we might look at what Mr E. R. Kelly, M.A., F.S.A., had to say some quarter of a century later:

Knodishall-cum-Buxlow is a parish and village 3½ miles south-east-by-east from Saxmundham and a mile south-west from Leiston station, in the Eastern division of the County, Blything hundred and union, Framlingham and Saxmundham county court district; rural deanery of Dunwich, south district, archdeanery of Suffolk and diocese of Norwich. The church of St. Lawrence consists of a chancel and nave, with tower of flint: the windows are partly stained: the interior is plain and stuccoed, and marked in imitation of stone, and in 1845 was renovated at the expense of the late Rev George Ayton Whitaker, M.A. who in 1838 built a vestry and the present excellent glebe house and offices: in 1878 the chancel roof was entirely renewed, and is now open-timbered; there is an old brass in the chancel wall, date 1400. The register dates from the year 1566. The living is a rectory, land tax redemmed, and the tithes were commuted in 1846 yearly, exclusive of the rent of 16 acres of glebe: it is in the gift of Mrs. Whitaker and held by the Rev. Hunting Jollye, M.A. of Jesus College, Cambridge; there are 63 acres of land in the parish exempt from tithes. Thomas and Richard Lee Mayhew, esquires are lords of the manors. The chief landowners in the parish are Captain Bloomfield, Lord Huntingfield, T. B. Wentworth esq, and H. Whitaker esq. with several small owners. The soil is good loam, but the eastern boundary approaching the sea is rather a light soil; subsoil chiefly clay and sand. The chief crops are wheat, barley and roots, and some land in pasture. The area is 1,772 acres; rateable value, £2,974, and the population in 1871 was 442. Buxlow was formerly a separate parish, but now part of Knodishall—The parish then became Knodishall-cum-Buxlow, but is commonly known as Knodishall. The Parish Clerk was Charles Barnes.

There were the usual number of farmers, but a Robert Norman had sprung up, described as "ironfounder, noted for chilled

ploughshares, all kinds kept in stock". Charles Nunn was a builder
and contractor, who sported an advertisement which states he was
established in 1855, and describes himself as an ecclesiastical
builder and contractor, who was able to supply waggons,
tumbrels, agricultural implements, etc. And the railway had
penetrated as far as Aldeburgh on a branch line, with a station at
Leiston, change at Saxmundham, which has but yesterday
become unprofitable and closed. It was certainly not there in
1855, or in 1850 when grandfather's taciturn brother Henry
married Rebecca Butcher, who I believe hailed from Pear Tree
Farm.

In those far away days when the only books they knew anything about were the Bible and Prayer Book (although Rebecca
may have become acquainted with the *Dairyman's Daughter*,
which was one of my mother's favourites), the Christian names
were Christian, so the girls were all Rebeccas, Naomis, Susannahs,
Marys, Ruths, Hannahs, Sophias, Rachaels, Mahalas; until you
didn't know which Rebecca was which, or whether Mahala was
sister, cousin, or aunt in that line. It was different with the boys,
because although named after prophets, priests and kings, either
major or minor, they also had nicknames, which usually described their shortcomings in no uncertain manner. This would
explain why my dear old round-faced great aunt came by her
name and my mother by hers.

I don't know how much of their married life was spent at
Knodishall-cum-Buxlow—whether Uncle Harry went there to
work, or whether it was the other way round—and Rebecca
came to Middleton-cum-Fordley, and never left it again. Of one
thing I am perfectly convinced, viz., that their life was a placid
stream that flowed on serenely to the end. I think Rebecca was
a dominant personality, more so than her spouse; but I do not
think so to unpleasantness. It was perhaps that Henry never
differed from her opinion. Certainly she didn't "thump him well
at eighty for what he had done at fourteen". But I don't
suppose there was a single spot in Middleton they didn't know,
even a pond or pulk, a path, a tree; and where houses or
cottages had been when squires and farmers thought more of a
sick cow than they did of the men who tended them.

There was one aspect of village life which had only just died into an unregretted past, that escaped both the *cum* villages. No record appears of any persecution of witches, although sixty were executed in Suffolk alone during a single year. The neighbouring county of Essex was more affected than any other English county. Poor lonely old souls would be suspected, accusations made and evidence accumulated. Someone would suffer a calamity in the livestock line, and the least defensive person would suffer blame. The poor creature might seek some neighbourly service only to be turned away empty handed. Village persecution, with no hope of escape, could be a terrible thing. I am sure old Aunt Rebecca would never have lent herself to that, she was too much a Christian.

Old Aunt Rebecca lived in the twilight of another day, and would recall the queer old houses in which she had lived and been 'larned' by the various mistresses. One of her tales was about the house where they kept a tame hedgehog in order to keep down the crickets and cockroaches that infested the place. And, of course, some mistresses would not have been slow in boxing a maid's ears, especially if she made a false stitch, on the principle of no gains without pains. One mistress was so handy that she would even box the master's ears, his offence when he grew older, being that he would jog the maid's elbow when she was giving him his darnick of brandy. But those were the days when if children behaved badly during service time in chapel or in church, they would be turned up and soundly whipped then and there, any crying being drowned by the singing. Moreover, she was a Sunday School teacher all her married life, and would have been in all probability indoctrinated by Dr Watts' verses, such as:

> The tulip and the butterfly
> Appear in gayer coats than I.
> Let me be dressed fine as I will
> Flies, worms and flowers excell me still.

I think both Uncle Harry and Aunt Rebecca never enjoyed ill health. On the other hand they looked on as others proliferated in imaginary complaints. I never heard any reference to their poor legs, chest or other parts of the body that were liable to give the most expressive twinges and opportunities for commiseration. After all life would have been rather flat without resort to certain remedies that had come down from a limited genealogy. I never heard of them calling at Broom's shop for a bottle of medicine, or keeping the remains of such a prescription on the top shelf of the pantry for next time. But I have no doubt that Rebecca, if not Harry, had sometimes entered into the delicious experiences of a death bed scene, gathering round the bed, watching the variations of breathing, colour or other infallible signs, sometimes to be shattered by the revival of the departing resuming duties the week following. Of course, such behaviour sometimes led to fatal consequences. However, I often wonder how they managed in their old age, since they had no offspring. There was no welfare state in those days, but I never heard a tale of melancholy. They managed somehow, possessed the salve of everlasting cheerfulness, had a bite or two in the larder, if they had no home-brewed on the beer stool. Neither did they seek or welcome any external aid, and as they were Methodists Rebecca would not have been eligible for red flannel petticoats or a new edition of the Prayer Book. But she would have had her class money ready when the minister came round with the tickets.

I think it was Harry who went first—which is much the better when male and female old age are considered. He had no obituary notice as he sank into the soil from whence he came, but he went to lie with his kith and kin on the south side of the dear old churchyard. But Rebecca followed soon after, and I have found an account of her passing, written by a namesake niece whom she had fostered. It was written to my father and mother.

Lavender Cottage,
Middleton Street.
Oct. 14, 1905.

My dear Lie and Ted.

I am just sending you a line to say poor old Aunt has entered into rest at last, she passed away about 20 to 12 this morning. She was conscious up to about 2 or 3 this morning but after then she took no notice, only difficulty in breathing. I think it was what one call a very hard death, but I trust it was peace within. She just slightly opened her eyes & I held her hand so if she could see me she knew I was there & then she drew one long breath & then all was still, her

Spirit was freed from earth. Poor old dear she wasn't much trouble to any one long was she?

She paid her rent on Wednesday & then was taken home. Wasn't it all wisely ordered. I don't expect we can keep her long because she is a full stomach but will let you know when we have decided on the day. Of course if you any of you wish to come we shall be pleased to see you at the same time I don't wish it if you can't, I quite understand. We must give the house up now & I spose have an auction, so if there is anything you would like you must let me know. We have to agree with her relations as well as between ourselves. I hope you will let Susie see this as it will spare me going over it again.

We are going to lock the poor body up tonight & go home to sleep it will be better than sleeping here. I am so glad Hannah have been here with me. Tell Susie if there is anything she wish for to let me know. I should have written to her only thought one of you could get out better than she can with a baby. I shall write to her next. Must say goodbye with love from us all, your loving sister

R. Barham.

Father say he think perhaps about Thursday, if you can manage it.

This was followed by another letter dated 17th October 1905, because the penny post in those days was reliable and swift:

I have just received your letter and I appreciate your kind offer to come, but *no* I do not mind one bit about your not coming. I quite understand it all & do not see the good of it only as you say to talk to. The weather is very cold here and you might get a cold & be laid up yourself, so I think it is wise not to come & your train fare will buy you a jacket.

I have to get a jacket & a hat, I have got a felt one. Hannah and I went to Leiston & got them yesterday. She is going home tonight to let Charlie come on Wednesday night, we have decided on Thursday at 2.30. It will be more convenient for everyone even if we have to screw her down tomorrow. She is changing a good deal. I have to go to Baylie (the doctor) & Turner for certificates, now I must go & speak to Mr. Hamilton (the Rector) & Pepper about Thursday & then bake a cake or two, but I shall be alright. I feel nicely well & sleep beautiful so does father, thank God. Mrs Marjoram is so nice to be with. (She lived to be a hundred and treated her daughters aged seventy as though they were young girls). I am not a bit nervous. I was in the house alone all day on Sunday. Father went to chapel & I was glad.

Your loving sister
R. Barham.

P.S.

I am glad about your bonnet. Mrs Woods ought to see that. She told Lou she liked yours.

Dear old Great Aunt Rebecca would have died in the same bed she had shared with Uncle Harry all their married life. It was a four-poster, hung round with curtains and valances, with straw palliasses over a webbed tarpaulin base, and on that one of the best goose feather beds that her housewifely skill had made when she was young. And at the head a little embroidered pocket was pinned, just big enough to take his turnip watch. How simple and satisfying was this cottage scheme of furnishing that never needed a renewal, since time in those lavender-scented days did not change.

I knew Lavender Cottage so well. It is all imprinted in my mind's eye, so named because it had a bush of that fragrant plant at the little old fashioned wooden door, that grew nearly as high as the door itself and penetrated the whole abode, not only the tiny rooms but the memory of them.

Not all her delightful country cottage home would have gone to auction. If it had it would only have realized a few shillings, because we have some of her linen sheets marked with little scarlet initials, and her coarsely woven blankets that helped to keep their poor old limbs warm before death chilled them. But Uncle Harry's wing chair, similar to the one in which grandfather reflected on life's passing years, disappeared; her Suffolk chair with the three little balls in the framework of the back went also. There was probably a scramble for the willow pattern china, the bit or two of Wedgwood, and the rat-tailed spoons. As for the four-poster with its lovely patchwork quilt made by a sister-in-law and given her as a wedding present, I think that must have gone to her relatives at Knodishall. I suppose the coco matting (pronounced cuckoo), must have got burnt up, although it was by no means worn out when I last saw it, and it smelt so nice and seemed to blend in with the scheme of things. But her pot plants would have found their way to other cottage windows. And, by the way, her bust of dear old John Wesley done by Ralph Wood was probably picked up by one of those wretched dealers that had begun to hang about cottage back doors.

The photograph (facing page 81) shows the old couple sitting outside their backhouse door, in front of the water butt, which in this case is made of brick and is filled at certain times by a rain-water pipe that slopes at an acute angle from the gutter at the front of the cottage down the end wall. Aunt is sitting on a Suffolk chair of which one can just see the back. They both peer at the funny old contraption which is taking the picture, wondering what on 'arth' he be a doin' on under the black cloth. The faces are a study in resignation and seriousness, but I think the exiguous wort on aunt's right cheek is really a flaw on the camera plate. And you will agree with me when I say that aunt's bombazine dress has never followed the trammels of fashion save on the day it was new. I wonder how many times it had taken her to chapel and home again. The same could be said of uncle with what looks like a vicuna waistcoat, a cloth much sought after in those days, since it never wore out and ended a greasy existence with the death of the owner. And I like his old linen slop with the bone buttons. I think the peeled stick between them was for telling the depth of water in the butt. Are they looking back into the past, or far away into the future?

She was a kindly shrewd old woman, not easily led away by a lot of old squit, neither was she amused when one of the preachers recounted the story of the Flood. The drowning people cried to Noah to take them in, "But Noah, he oped the winder, an' he say tew 'em, he saay, 'Bor, I dussent! I've had orders to the contrary.'"

3. UNCLE FRANK

We men, who in our morn of youth defied
The elements, must vanish;—be it so.

Once upon a time when frugality was endemic to life, children were encouraged to save their pennies in a toy pottery house. I have one such, sans chimney pots, three windows above with

Uncle Frank

Valley Farm, Middleton-cum-Fordley

white outlined sash-bars, a white dotted string course below and two arched windows that flank an important-looking gabled doorway. And, yes, there is a tiny white knob to the door. The slot for the money is in the roof, but how it was extracted is a complete mystery, particularly if you were very young. Sometimes these intriguing ornaments inveigled young Methodists into saving money in order to build a new chapel.

The photograph (facing page 96) of this compact piece of domestic architecture, still to be found in Middleton-cum-Fordley, might have provided the ideal design for such a hoarding place, because it looks for all the world as a money-box house.

It is known as Hill House because on a hill it stands—in a countryside proverbially flat, yet it is on a level with the top of the church spire. I am not so sure though, that if the latter had retained its golden cockerel that was supposed to give warning when the devil was about, whether heights might not have been altered. Moreover, it is near the turnpike that runs from Yoxford to Leiston and Aldeburgh, which always has something a clattering along it, even perhaps a gypsy family with their travelling house trailing smoke, on the way to or from the moor. A little way over northwards, still standing high, is Trust Farm, and beyond that was Sam Self's farm beside the Packway. Everywhere is as old as old can be and as quiet as a mouse. The scene is begirt with trees, and every little water bank is spangled with primroses and violets. Yes, it is quiet, but if you have time to stand and listen, you may catch the sound of Ted Foulsham's anvil as he is beating out shoes for the local farmers' 'hosses'.

As you will gather from the picture, it is a small holding, a sort of one-horse farm, with more to it at the back than in the front, although the outhouses of excoriated red brick and tiles line up beside the yard at the side. Uncle Frank has brought up Daisy and Buttercup to be included in the picture because they are distinctly part of the family. He has a good hold of Daisy but has tied up Buttercup to the nice little bit of white-painted fence. She fancies she can see 'suffen tew ate' on the garden side. But there, all the best bits in life are out of reach. The young woman at the gate wearing those leg-o'-mutton sleeves is his daughter Mariah, and the astonishing thing to note is that the

7

front door is wide open and two windows above to let in a little of that lovely Suffolk air. How very unusual to be sure.

> Sweet Spring, full of sweet dayes and roses,
> A box where sweets compacted lye.

Now Uncle Frank was a Barham, number nine in the tree of that numerous family that populated the village from the very beginning of the nineteenth century onwards. Then, since everyone was related to one another, they were always known by their Christian names to the boys and girls that were their descendants. His wife was Clara, coming from as far away as the next village of Westleton. They were a delightful pair, she with long tapering hands that could bake and brew, sew and contrive; always wearing a little old black lace cap, hair parted in the middle, and with a singing voice like that of a robin's. When they sang "We're marching on to Emmanuel's land", and kept on marching, she would come in with a step or two behind, like an echo. It was the same with "Lo! He comes with clouds descending"; her clouds were a bit later than the others.

Frank wears his fragrant-smelling old clothes, corduroy trousers and black felt hat that may have been made from Brandon rabbit skins. Clara must have gone to heaven years before this picture was taken, and he is now leading a kind of supernumerary existence, living with his daughter, turning his hand to just that bit of work which he knows so well how to do. I don't suppose he ever strayed further than Saxmundham or Wickham Market on market days, or maybe Dunwich for a chapel frolic; and then he would have been right glad to get home to his Clara, because it was the best thing he ever did when he married her.

As he was born in 1822 and this picture was taken in the nineties, he would have been in his seventies. Think what that meant: a farmer's boy through all those wonderful years before Queen Victoria came to the throne, when squires ruled almost as feudal lords and parsons followed hard after. There were a number of villages where the curfew was still rung, and at nearby Bramfield a busy old rector had continued to collect the poll tax of 4d. a head, levied in the reign of Richard II, until 1805, when it was dropped by the opposition of one of the village Hampdens, named Page. But it was a good life as Uncle Frank's benevolent face testified, although wages for a married man were only 10s. a week, poverty was immanent and pain difficult to alleviate.

I don't know where in the parish Uncle Frank lived his life, and had his children—who were all well brought up and as benevolent as himself and his Clara. It would have been at one of the farms scattered about, perchance Valley Farm, down there by the sunken sandy way that was impassable in winter. Or Moor Farm, that has such a beautiful Tudor gable end that faces the turnpike. Maybe it was the Dove House, that I always think of as being that colour, although it was pink-washed. But it was rarely out of the way and a long way from the chapel, particularly so in winter. It might even have been the Yew Tree Farm, near the spot where the Barham family began; or Hawthorn Farm, so named from trees both red and white, where they had an old dog that barked the whole night through when there was a full moon. Or it might have been Potash Farm, or even the Water Mill Farm that had a footpath running by it, leading to the railway that he could remember being built.

Like all his relatives he was a Methodist, and one can imagine him going down the hill on the Sabbath to sing the old hymns in the square-faced chapel. He could even remember when it was built by willing hands, for he was 6 years old when it was opened. What a wonderful event that was, surely he could never forget, and the burst of excitement it caused. It was whooly dark at that old chapel corner and the wind whistled there fit to cut you in half. But it was warm inside. Later on, in dark days, they used to stick an old oil lamp outside in a case; but it had a bad and evil habit of going out when it was most needed.

It may well have been that someone was at that chapel opening who had listened to Wesley when he visited Yarmouth, for the great man was there in 1790, just five months before his death, and this is what he wrote in his journal: "Thursday, 14th. October, 1790 I went to Yarmouth and at length found a society in peace, and much united together. In the evening the congregation was much too large to get into the preaching-house; but they were far less noisy than usual. After supper, a little company went to prayer; and the power of God fell upon us, especially when a young woman broke out in prayer, to the surprise and comfort of us all."

I don't know when Uncle Frank died but he may have lived long enough to see the first ever motor-car come into the village. It spluttered along, a regular rat-trap of a thing, and stopped dead just outside the school. All the scholars, a round hundred of them, were allowed out to see this great sight. Unfortunately the owner used such bad language at the driver because he couldn't get the 'duzzy' thing to budge, that they were hurriedly taken inside again, lest their morals should be corrupted.

Uncle Frank, with his Clara, lies somewhere in that crowded little churchyard, under the steeple that was his lodestar. Around are so many other Barhams, husbandmen all, a faithful brotherhood, active as it were in the life of the living, and never to be forgotten.

> Enough, if something from *their* hands have power
> To live, and act, and serve the future hour.

4. VALLEY FARM

I have cause to remember Valley Farm because when I was very small it was my job to go there to collect the milk. To do that one had to thread a way alongside old overgrown hedges alive with birds and sweet-smelling flowers, especially honeysuckle; and to be caught up suddenly by another almost momentary perfume, as though someone had just opened a scent bottle, let the air escape and replaced the stopper. To my small nose there was nothing so sweet as Suffolk flowers. It was sweet briar, and with a touch of magic joy one stopped to try and recapture it once again. Was it this bit of quickset or that?

At that time the farm was kept by Robert Stannard and his wife Bessy, who was the daughter of Uncle Frank and the sister of Mariah. Poor Mariah died young of cancer, but Bessy lived on to a good old age, as pleasant a Barham as any of the others. Robert hailed from Dunwich.

The picture of the old farmhouse (facing page 97), shows the complete family standing in the sanded driveway, which was circular to allow a carriage to call at the front door and pass out along the gravelled path. Bob is in his field boots, wearing a quite respectable bowler hat; Bessy has a full length dress, with leg-ofmutton sleeves, hands carefully clasped; the little girl with that splendid pinafore, whiter than white, is another Bessy. Even the dog knows it is having its photo taken and is content to pose hoping they will all come out well in the picture.

The house itself is old, covered with its original thatch, but has obviously undergone a restoration, because the low window at the gable end is a sash. The others also are replacements with their wooden bars, because the original would have been diamond panes, with glass almost like horn. But how neat and nice they look, all duly closed as you will not fail to notice, and fitted with little white linen blinds, like those at my grandmother's. There was no need for dark colours, because the air was so sweet and clean. Note too the neat little drip-board over the windows, acting almost like an eyebrow, and that there is no guttering to the steeply pitched roof. Neither was there a damp-course, so that the base of the walls have been treated with tar. I like too, the typical unambitious front entrance with its classical surround and recessed white door, which unlike those of the cottage homes, seems as though it might be used. But normally, if you wanted to see Bessy Stannard, or even go there to tea, you would make your way over a cobbled path to the back door.

But there is more to it than that, Bob Stannard was not the owner. He was the steward and ran the farm for someone else. In the summer months it was let to visitors, so that Bob, the two Bessys and the dog, lived at the back part. And the visitors were regaled with Bessy's cooking. Moreover, it was a farm of some importance and in 1879 was run by Frederick Charles Bendall, who may well have been the collector of those bits of masonry that are lined up under the windows. They intrigue me very much, because they speak so loudly of the far-away historic Suffolk, of which the farmhouse is a relic.

The round stone object was probably a cannon ball, possibly hurled ashore in some old sea fight just off that bit of coast, when they used such things. Of the others there could be any one of three sources. They may have come from Leiston Abbey when the chapel was turned into a barn and the monks had ceased to chant loudly or slowly. Even that old ruined abbey just off that turnpike road to the east, was a replacement, the original being nearer the sea. Secondly, as per the preacher, they may have come from the abbey at Sibton, the only Cistercian house in the county. Or thirdly, from the old parish church, the one of the two in the churchyard that had been demolished to let the other hold its services in peace. Do you think that Frederick Charles went about with his eyes open, and a charm was blown on his own thoughts when he saw such pieces lying about in neighbouring farmyards? I wonder.

Valley Farm was always well stocked. There were outhouses all round the stackyard, full of animals giving vent to their particular expressions; chickens in and out all over the place, especially the barn if the doors were open; and often lovely corn stacks creating a barrier between one and the dairy door. Bessy was a first-class farmer's wife; she made such lovely butter, as yellow as a cowslip and something to remember if you had it with Aunt Rebecca's rusks, a slice of brick-oven-baked bread, or even Westbrook's bread from Leiston. Bread was bread in those days, even if it did come from a shop that smelt of dough and yeast. And if Bessy baked on a Friday, she churned on a Tuesday, and was sometimes rarely out put because the butter wouldn't 'come'. Eggs of course, were there in plenty, and if you went for a dozen (a penny each) you would get thirteen, lovely brown eggs, each done up in a separate little bit of paper so they wouldn't break easily. You took a nice little, pretty little, wicker basket for those that even in its weaving seemed to declare it was as Suffolk as the fowls that laid the eggs or the cows that yielded the milk. People really lived in those days and I don't wonder they suffered with gout.

Valley Farm, as its name implies, is in a hollow. Not by a watercourse, but at the bottom of a bit of a rise that goes up to Hill Farm westwards and to Theberton eastwards. A sandy lane flanked it on the eastward side, the sort of sunken road that figured so largely in Flanders in the First Great War. This was really a portion of an old packway, almost impassable at any time of the year. So to reach the farmyard from the north you climbed up to a field path that was sometimes waist high in the most lovely golden corn you ever saw, grown with the aid of Nature's own fertiliser. It was a sight in blazing sun, with here and there a poppy, or here and there a corn blue bottle or the rich purple corn cockle; or again under a full moon, a moon that was so much bigger than the one that shone in our suburban sky. And yet, in the deep peace might come a cry of distress, a poor old rabbit caught in a trap. How I dreaded those sounds.

Bessy loved her old chapel in the bosom of which she had been nourished, and, like so many others, clung to the past when the Barhams, the Buttons and all the others helped to build it brick by brick. Those days instilled into her by both father and mother were always the best days, and perchance she may have caught her breath as she realized they were never to come again. But whereas other mawthers like my mother had entered the great metropolis 'by land' as the saying went in the early days of railway travelling, she had stayed at home. Whether she went to the church school under Mistress Ann Arnold, or the one my mother and aunt attended, run by Mrs Davey (although it was old snuff-taking Mr Davey who gets the credit for it in the directory), I wouldn't know; but she certainly 'larned' how to read and write, cook and sew, and contrive, add up as far as a dozen eggs, a pound of butter and a gallon of milk, and be a farmer's wife.

She would have qualified for the little bit of 'poo-et-ry' to be found on a Sunderland Jug:

THE GOOD WIFE
Show me the wife that's on the watch,
For every little rent, or scratch,
And cures it with a timely patch,
    Before you know it;
She is a woman fit to match
    A Lord or Poet.

5. TAKEN IN THE NINETIES

As a companion piece to Valley Farm we might have a look at a study of undisturbed yesterday, taken about the turn of the century (facing page 112). Everything has been allowed to grow and hustle along in its own sweet way. Presumably it is off the main road, has a bit of a pightle (a small enclosed field) in front and nothing changed; even the blackberry bush trailing over the slatted fence will yield a bit of fruit to mingle with the apples in the orchard come the autumn. But what a feast of glory will be granted in that same season of the year, when the green of the creeper turns to gold. Was it all taken for granted, or were some hearts gladdened? However, this photograph was taken when fields and roadsides had very tall fences (hedges) trailed over by all sorts of flowers, and when one went to church by lanes filled with roses.

The picture is of a mother and her five daughters, the youngest of whom is very much in the fashion, wearing clothes possibly obtained from Mr Footman of Waterloo House, Ipswich. (The youngest daughter always was the pampered one.) Mother remains in the past, with her white apron neckerchief and plastered hair, the only hair style of those days. They are all there, the parrot has been brought out to enjoy the sun and be in the party. Fluff is in the foreground, as shaggy as the grass, and Tibby is in the arms of the daughter on the left. The most remarkable thing is that the windows are all open except those on the ground floor; but as the doors are wide open, enough of the sweet-scented air can enter. That they are well up-to-date is evidenced by the room left of the door on the right, which has a blind with a fringe of lace. That was considered 'it' in those days; the deeper the more fashionable. And note how the windows are crowded with pot plants.

But how would you like to sleep in one of those bedrooms, where the sun came peeping in at morn? Your rest in the mornings would have been disturbed by birds nestling in that deep growth, and there might have been a few insects creeping in and out of the crevices of the wall paper, especially silver fish. But you took that sort of thing for granted. There is no gutter to the mansard roof with its splendid array of tiles, and it won't be long before the green mantle creeps further and further upwards. The time of day must be in the afternoon, when all the work was done and all were wearing their Sunday best, but the picture would have been sadly incomplete without that nice old cleft paling fence; it sort of shuts them in their dear old home, of which they are so proud.

One cannot see the furnishings within or smell the lovely smell that pervaded all from the dimity in the bedrooms to the coco-matting and the bit of Brussels carpet in the keeping room. There

would have been Suffolk chairs with shiny seats to sit upon, and
a grandfather near the fireplace. A capacious corner cupboard
that held all kinds of things in the way of bottles, including
embrocation, medicine and home-made wines, not forgetting
cowslip. A clock ticking a slower march than in these hurried
days, and a four-poster bed upstairs with a white coverlet, or
patchwork quilt that fairly shone and sparkled with delicious bits
of silk of other years and wealthier owners. It might have been a
feudal England, but everyone worked with a will, and they didn't
have strikes every other day. They might even have read this in
their county paper: "East Bergholt, 1880. Marvellous Harvest
Performance. A man named Isaac Woolard, who lives at East End,
a hawker by trade, contracted with Mr. Welham, a farmer, of
this parish, to cut down with the scythe 22 acres of wheat for £10.
Woolard, a very little man, accomplished the feat in 10 days, and
in the meantime went to Colchester, and bought two cottages by
public auction. The wheat has been thrashed, and realised 166
sacks. Under ordinary circumstances a harvestman would have
taken four or five weeks to have completed the above task."
Even mother could not have remembered the agrarian riots,
neither could any of them see the Great War coming that was to
change it all.

The photograph may well have been taken in the month of
June because of the lush growth, when the flowers were out, the
thrushes singing their madrigals, and the blackbirds throating
their joy of living. One can almost hear the cuckoo's voice in the
distance, on the far side of the ten-acre (the note is always in the
distance like the rainbow's end). Moreover, I would suggest that
the old Queen, the mother of her people, is still on the throne and
that her flag is flying from the round tower at Windsor.

How strange is the march of time when passages such as this
can appear in our daily papers:

Flower meadows are vanishing so fast that in eastern counties
nature lovers are buying them so that they can show their children
what the countryside used to look like.

The Suffolk Trust for Nature Conservation has paid £2,217 for
328 acres of fenland, unchanged for 1,000 years. Once free grazing
land for the poor, it has sedges, rushes and wild orchids.

In North Bedfordshire, the Bedfordshire and Huntingdon

Naturalists' Trust is negotiating to buy a cowslip meadow. A joint chairman said that the cowslip was disappearing as a result of the use of selective weed killer. The buttercup was also dwindling.

"We are trying to buy a meadow that has cowslips still, so that the future generations can see what a field of cowslips looks like."

The Lincolnshire Trust for Nature Conservation has acquired for £1,200 three small meadows at Bratoft, East Lincs, where cowslips, wild orchids, small broom, adder's tongue fern, buttercups and other rarer plants grow.

The Cambridgeshire and Isle of Ely Naturalists' Trust has paid £6,500 for a few hundred acres of the Ouse washes, flood meadows where fringed water lilies grow in the ditches.

It has also leased 30 acres of cowslip meadow at Fulbourd, Cambs, as an educational nature reserve. The chairman of the trust's executive said: "In 10 years time there may well be hardly any cowslips left in our part of eastern England. Where you have intensive arable farming, meadows in the main survive only around villages.

"The meadows will go for new housing or be ploughed up by farmers, or improved with nitrogenous fertilisers which make the grass grow longer for the cattle, and by competition kill off the cowslips.

"I would like to see every parish in our country have a small piece of meadow where there will be some wild flowers. Unless we do this, the sight of a meadow full of buttercups and daisies may become a thing of the past in our part of the world."

Back to our picture, cowslip and buttercup meadows were all around that old homestead. They had cows named after those very petals. How far away is the village, I wonder? And how distant the next-door neighbour? They would have been within hail of the church bell. I wonder if they could see the mossed and lichened steeple, or whether it is hid by trees, or a fold in the landscape. Time passed over that spot with a caressing hand, but one day perhaps, the old home became but a memory. Did some of them ever come back:

> And, many a year elaps'd, return to view
> Where once the cottage stood, the hawthorn grew—
> Remembrance wakes with all her busy train,
> Swells at my breast, and turns the past to pain.

6. RAFE'S MILL

I have just come across an old photograph (facing page 113) of a very fine mill that was working in full order in my grandfather's day, and which he would have known quite well. As Westleton, the adjacent parish across the water splash to his own, had two working mills, they were known by their owner's names—at least this one was, and by the old English rendering of his name, because Ralphs in those days were Rafes, and it was Sir Rafe Blois, not Sir Ralph, who lived at Cockfield Hall, Yoxford.

I do not know if Robert Ralph built the mill that assumed his name for the rest of its life, in fact I do not think he did because his name does not appear in White's Directory, but it does in Kelly's for 1879. However, the millers in 1855 are an interesting local lot. James Rous was a corn, flour, seed and coal merchant, and tax collector, so he in his very local name played many parts; and John and Joseph Balls were corn millers. But the name that intrigues me is that of Susan Oclee.

We have been led to believe that women have only recently become free and independent beings. But as far as my researches go they seem to have been with it since the days of Domesday, or even earlier—witness Boadicea. They appear in the lists as farmers, shoemakers, innkeepers, blacksmiths and wheelwrights; besides being the stronger sex in more ways than one. Did not Adam blame it all on Eve in the very first instance? Of course I can't be quite sure that this was Susan's mill, because at one time Westleton had three mills, including a post mill, as black as Satan, that stood at the top of the hill as you go to Dunwich and which has been recently demolished. It was complete with round house. There was another post mill with open base, standing on three brick piers just north of Rafe's tower mill. The brick piers are still there, but the miller's house has gone. This old relic, because it must have been one of Westleton's first mills, always reminded me of those old rickety structures to be found in France and Flanders in the earlier days of the First World War, before they were blown to pieces because of their use as look-outs. They seemed strangely reminiscent of illustrations to *Don Quixote*, in which the poor deranged upholder of chivalry tried his hand at tilting with them. After all, if the Knight of the Sorrowful Countenance came on a crusade at the time of year when Susan Oclee kept her mill in trim he might have thought she was an English Dulcinea del Toboso, and acted accordingly.

Windmills had their use in warfare long before 1914, because Henry III was reputed to have hid in one after the battle of Lewes in 1264. Edward III is thought to have watched the fight at Crecy from one in 1346. (Neither should we forget that he set sail for that expedition from the Suffolk port of Goseford in the Deben.) The mill in question which had walls seven feet thick, was only demolished in 1887. Then Charles I watched his first repulse from a windmill at Naseby in 1645. These would all have been post mills, a type said to have been invented in Flanders, with canvas sails or whips.

But let us have another look at that picturesque and lovely structure, a masterpiece of mechanical farming and beautiful adjunct of any village. The small domed-top clap-board building, to match the top cap of the mill is a superb piece of carpentry. (There were two kinds of these caps, one was the round or Dutch cap, the other was English, rather like a Scotch cap, whereby is an anomaly.) It may have held an engine for use when there was a dead calm. It has nearly all gone now, but some of the old outhouses remain, and the comfortable mill house, with its squint window that looks out to sea and which may or may not have been connected with smuggling. You must realize that from this spot the weather was watched in a far keener manner, and was known by a deeper instinct than anything that comes to us via radio or television. How oncoming storms would be dreaded lest harm came, and how clouds of rain would be received with gratitude after weeks or even months of drought, reflected in drooping crops.

Was Rafe's Mill the one Susan Oclee kept and tended? Did she have to scramble out of bed when a storm burst, and race to attend to the sails if fierce winds were coming from a dangerous quarter? Certainly she would have known the difference between flour, middlings and bran. (When I kept rabbits as a boy in Southeast London, I often wondered at the names.) Did she make the best blackberry puddings for miles around, since they grew to perfection thereabouts, and her flour was so good? Possibly she sold the best honey distilled and alchemized from the wide spreading heath-covered common. Perchance she cooked her chickens in a large iron saucepan, and her scones in a frying pan over an open fire. But those were the days when you could get home-made bullseyes once a week at Eliza Marjoram's shop and, when Phoebe Thirkettle was a straw-hat maker.

Suffolk has long been famous for its windmills. What a wonderful picture the countryside must have presented when all the mills were working, when every village had its mill, sometimes two, three or even four—glistening under a Suffolk sky and turning in the wind that for ever blows; creating, as it were, a magic link of communication between parish and parish. William Cobbett, who visited Ipswich in 1830, gives something of the scene: "Immense quantities of flower are sent from this town. The windmills on the hills are so numerous that I counted whilst standing in one place, no less than seventeen. They are all painted or washed white, the sails are black, it was a fine morning, the wind was brisk and the twirling together added greatly to the beauty of the scene, which, having the broad and beautiful arm of the sea on one hand and the fields and meadows studded with farmhouses on the other, appeared to me the most beautiful sight of the kind I had ever beheld." (You can see these old mills depicted on early maps of Ipswich.)

In the old days most windmills had cloth sails, which were difficult and dangerous to deal with, especially in sudden winds. These were superseded by the patent or spring sails which were invented by an Ipswich engineer, Sir William Cubitt, who in 1807 introduced the vaned sail.

The story of these Suffolk windmills is long and distinguished, beginning with what is probably the earliest reference to such in our literature. It occurs in the celebrated *Chronicles of Jocelin of Brakelond*:

Herbert the dean erected a windmill upon Haberdon [high ground near Bury St Edmunds]. When the abbot heard of this, his anger was so kindled that he would scarcely eat or utter a single word. On the morrow, after hearing mass, he commanded the sacrist that without delay he should send his carpenters thither and overturn it altogether, and carefully put by the wooden materials in safe keeping.

The dean, hearing this, came to him saying that he was able in law to do this upon his own frank fee, and that the benefit of the wind ought not to be denied to anyone. He further said that he only wanted to grind his own corn there and nobody's else's, lest it should be imagined that he did this to the damage of the neighbouring mills. The abbot, his anger not yet appeased, answered, "I give you as many thanks as if you had cut off both my feet; by the mouth of God I will not eat bread until that building be plucked down. You are an old man, and you should have known that it is not lawful even for the King or his justiciary to alter or appoint a single thing without the banlieue, without the permission of the abbot and convent; and why have you presumed to do such a thing? Nor could I endure that the mill of our cellarer, lately set up, should stand, except that it was erected before I was abbot. Begone", he said, "begone; before you have come to your house, you shall hear what has befallen your mill."

But the dean being afraid before the face of the abbot, by the counsel of his son, Master Stephen, forestalled the servants of the sacrist, and without delay caused that very mill which had been erected by his own servants to be overthrown. So that when the servants of the sacrist came thither, they found nothing to be pulled down.

The Suffolk windmills included the unique example of the ring-sailed mill at Haverhill, now demolished, which was thought to have been the forerunner of the American wind-pumps. And northwards along the coast was the tallest mill ever built in this country, at Yarmouth, standing 120 feet high. All the mills in East Suffolk were right-handed but those in Cambridgeshire were left. In the old days the miller had to turn his mill into the wind by pushing or levering it by hand, but in 1750 Andrew Meikle introduced the fantail, which made the mill self-adjusting. The stone track or wind track in the case of post mills, on which the turn was made, was of 2-inch-thick elm planks, embedded in the ground, and this circle can still be traced in the case of the derelict specimen at Westleton.

Although the decline and demolition of the Suffolk mills began in the early years of this century, a large number survived until the First World War, and a few until the advent of the second. The tale of their eclipse is much the same in every case: cost of upkeep, or getting tail winded—that is to say damaged internally by the wind getting behind the sails, which could happen if the wind changed suddenly in a gale and the fliers did not respond quickly enough in turning the mill. In the case of tower mills this meant that the cap was blown off, and with post windmills the sails. When one considers that it took 5 hundredweight of white lead paint to cover an ordinary post windmill, together with the cost of internal and external repairs, one realizes how much courage was required to keep a mill in running order. One thing stands out and that was the love which those old mills evoked in the hearts of those who inherited them. Often enough an old miller would say he had no use for her (a mill, like a ship is always spoken of as 'she'), she could be pulled down or destroyed by fire. Yet the next moment he might say that anybody could work a mill, but not everyone could handle her.

The Friston mill was run by the Wright family for many generations. She was restored about 1950, and fitted with a new set of apple teeth to the driving wheel, but Mr Wright told me then that "she hugs a bit when she starts". She is now in queer street but may yet be preserved, being one of the tallest of mills. Mr Wright further told me that when he was a young man seven other mills could be seen at work from his upper floor; and one of his especial memories was of noting the Aldeburgh mill (pulled down in 1924), 3 miles distant, driving in an opposite direction from his own. Whereas the Friston mill was driving from the north-west, that of Aldeburgh was working south-east, taking the wind from the water, while Friston's came from the land. But what of the space between he asked? His companion at the time, a much older man, had seen such an occurrence only once before in his life.

The mill at Saxtead Green, a wonderful sight in a new coat of paint, is now maintained as a national monument. And twenty years ago there lived there one Jesse Wightman, a millwright, who could dress the stones into a pattern that must have come down from an ancient civilization. Not far removed is Framsden mill, which has just been restored into working order by a few enthusiasts. A tale is told, that a youth, for a wager essayed to hold on to one of the sails and be carried round for one sweep. He was successful and survived.

Pakenham, to the north-east of Bury St Edmunds, has the finest mill in the county. It is a tower mill, a study in black and white, still working, the pride of the Bryant family. In this instance, one realizes the old millers were men of substance, with a huge yard full of pigs, geese, turkeys, ducks, chickens and even horses.

It is difficult today for us to realize how beautiful and friendly a windmill was, making certain sounds peculiar to itself when in work. The corn was fed to the stone from a shoe, which was a long shallow box, pivoted at one end, on top of the vat that held the stones, and sloping slightly downwards. When rattled by a 'damsel', which was a piece of iron fitted on to the bridge carrying the upper stone so that it revolved with the latter, the vibration set up made the corn travel along the shoe and fall into the eye of one stone. The clatter of the damsel against the shoe made the characteristic sound connected with a windmill. Other sounds were the thunderous roar made by the revolving stones and the swish and creak of the sails as they passed, each sail making its own characteristic sound.

Indeed, a mill was full of ingenious gadgets. One was the tell-tale, to warn the miller that the supply of corn to the stones was running down. This was devised with a piece of leather that had a hole in the centre of it through which a cord passed, having a knot below. The cord passed over a pulley fixed on the roof above the hopper and held up a bell. When the leather was buried in the corn in the hopper the continual downward action of the corn leaving the hopper, and that being supplied from the bin in the floor above, kept the leather buried and the bell up. When there was no more corn coming down the shute, the leather escaped, allowing the bell to fall and catch the spokes of the wheel above which it was suspended. The ringing warned the miller that the stones would soon run dry and cause a fire.

With the disappearance of the windmill, that wonderful race of old millwrights went also. They were practically masters of all trades and could work in wood, stone and iron. Morever, they knew something of ropes and tackle, because putting up a pair of sails into position, especially in wind, was no easy matter—but they could do it and think themselves none the better for accomplishing what was their job.

The tower that once was Shotley mill was hung with new sails fitted to it in the '70s of last century. They had been put up but not properly secured. The men went to Shotley Boot for a drink,

A woman and her daughters, photographed in the 1890s

Rafe's Mill, Westleton

Blythburgh
Church in an
Oxford frame

and whilst there a wind sprang up, caught the sails and broke them off. This ruined the miller (presumably Robert Rivers), and the mill was never used again.

Artists too often have been fooled when painting a mill. For example, the angle of the face of the sail vanes varies from the centre towards the end. This gives the characteristic feathering or twist that artists fail to represent. Moreover, the sails were parallel, or in some cases reduced in width towards the ends, but often the painter shows them much wider at the tips than at the centre.

Undoubtedly some of the merit of those great English scenes painted by Constable can be attributed to his early life in a windmill, when he watched the changing sky with an interest other than that of a miller. But the words of his younger brother remain: "When I look at a mill painted by John, I see that it will go round."

To end this, we might notice the attitude of some of those tight-fisted farmers when mills were at work: "A farmer at Stradbroke stocked the produce of five acres of wheat, and made a vow that it should never be thrashed while wheat was under 40s a comb. The owner died, when only twenty comb were obtained, the rest had been eaten by vermin. Two wreaths made from the stack were placed on his grave."

And this one, appearing as late as about 1925. "In the stackyard at Mr. W. Meen's farm at Stradbroke, there is a stack of wheat which has a remarkable history. It was built in 1873, and the owner made a vow that he would never thrash it until it realized 25s. a sack, a price which has never been offered. The stack stands on an iron support two feet from the ground, and is in an excellent state of preservation, being free from mice and rats. Recently some of the ears of wheat were pulled out, and the grains were found to be quite bright, though reddened with age. It is estimated that the stack contains 250 bushels."

7. THE CORNER OF A SUFFOLK VILLAGE

If you delve into the story of Suffolk villages you come across passages such as this, describing the church: "The magnificent single hammer-beam roof of the nave has a span of 17ft. 6ins.

8

is in ten bays and must be one of the richest in existence." This is not the vapid outburst of some infatuated sightseer but the sober truth as stated by a professional man, with regard to the church of St Mary, Earl Stonham.

It was my good fortune recently to be loaned an album of Suffolk scenes and newspaper cuttings made last century, when I came across the old photograph (facing page 160). I was immediately caught up by its fragrant peace and wondered if it could possibly be a product of an old camera, or was a Constable sketch because of its artless beauty. It is a bit of old Suffolk as it was a century ago, because the picture dates from about the '70s of that era. It is all so naturally beautiful without a trace of falseness, from the ivy-mantled chimney stack, to the broken rail of the fence, and the boy in his country clothes and hat. It is a curious and wonderful piece of reality that a boy, or girl for that matter, is always available to add a touch of nature that makes all the world akin. He stands there, pigeon-toed, a period piece as much as any other detail of the scene.

I wonder if the L-shaped farmhouse is still there? If so, I suppose the thatch has given place to tiles, or even slates. Certainly it is in need of a little attention, but blinks softly over the tiny bedroom windows. And has the parlour window still got those pretty bars that portion off the sunlight into no less than eighteen pieces? There does not seem very much provision for an opening to let in the air; but there, as grandmother would have said, there's plenty of that coming from the half-hatch door at the back. Next, following the frontage downwards, hidden by the vegetation, is the door; but how you reach it I wouldn't know. Neither do I know the species of the old tree with its gnarled trunk. It looks like some giant guardsman's hat as worn at Waterloo, or before, standing sentinel over old walls that were built when Armadas threatened our shores. And all the years between, morning and evening, day following day in endless succession, whereas the boy is surely peering into the future watching the man disappearing under the black cloth.

Across the way is the barn, thatched like the house, but with tarred wooden walls. I think the white patch by the side must be a gateway, possibly into the stackyard. The lane leads us on to that perfect outline, a labourer's cottage, with its tall brick chimney, which as it is high summer gives out no smoke. Although the house is thatched like all the others, the lean-to is not, being covered with those old mellowed red pantiles, product of a local brick kiln. But I really think that the round thing in the distance is the village pound. As it is circular, what else can it be? While the ragged bit of white between the end of the barn and the trees is the sky, and not a smudge on the plate made by the photographer when he coated it with film. This is a composition which Constable would have known and Birket Foster delighted to portray. Neither would either of them have had need to use any artistic licence.

This is Rectory Lane at Earl Stonham, so presumably it led also to the abode of one of Suffolk's fat livings, valued at £659, with parsonage house and 33 acres of glebe, in the gift of Pembroke College, Cambridge, and held by the Reverend Joseph Castley, M.A., formerly fellow and lecturer of that college.

Let me give you a description of the village as recorded in White's Directory for 1855:

Stonham (Earl) a parish of scattered houses, about 5 miles E. of Stowmarket, and 1 mile S.W. of the Post Office at Stonham Parva, contains 878 inhabitants [they had shrunk to 685 by 1871], and 2520 acres, 3 r, 31 p. of strong clayey land. Messrs Holmes, Jackson and Sparke of Bury St. Edmunds are lords of the manor, which is mostly freehold, and belongs chiefly to the Welham, Garnham, Matthew, Cathcart, Nunn, Plowman, Howlett, and a few other families. It anciently belonged to the Earls of Norfolk, and from them was called Earl Stonham, to distinguish from the two neighbouring Stonhams. The Duke of Norfolk had the grant of a market and fair here in the Ist. of Edward III, but they have been obsolete several centuries. Deerbolts Hall [note the name], now a farm house, was the seat of the Driver family. . . .

A close called Blunt's (3 A. 1 r. 2 P.) and Acre Meadow, in the manor of Filiol, in Earl Stonham, were settled in the 19th. of Edward 4th. in trust for the common benefit of the parishioners. George Reeve, in the 42nd. of Elizabeth, settled in trustees 20 A of land in Stowmarket and Stowupland for maintaining a schoolmaster to teach poor children of Earl Stonham. At the same time the Hall field (7 A.) was settled for apprenticing and buying books for the poor scholars, and the Mill field (6 A.), for the use of the poor. A messuage and 3 A of land called Dunham's, were settled, in the

15th. of Henry 8th. for the benefit of the parishioners. For the same purpose, the Guildhall (now the schoolroom) and a barn and 20 A. called Thradstones, near Stowmarket, were settled in the 15th. of Edward 4th., Burnt House land (8 A) was purchased in 1681, for the use of the parish, with sundry benefactions and money arising from the sale of wood. These Charity Estates, with some other land, purchased for and appropriated to the general use of the parishioners, are partly freehold and partly copyhold, and are under the direction of certain feofees, and the churchwardens for the time being. They comprise altogether about 64 acres, let for about £150, a year. The rents are carried to the same general account, and applied partly in paying a salary of £40 to the schoolmaster, who teaches eight free scholars; in providing about £9 worth of clothes for the free scholars; in buying gowns for two poor women; and in distributing about £30 among poor parishioners; and the rest of the income, after paying quit rents and various contingent expenses, is applied towards the expenses of the churchwardens, constable &c.

In those days Henry Brooks and William Gostling were corn millers. Robert Buck was at the 'Angel', Benjamin Colman the free schoolmaster, Leonard Doe baker and beerhouse keeper, William Hall carpenter and parish clerk, Robert Pells an iron founder, William Rush bricklayer, Josiah Ungless carpenter, Charles Warren wheelwright, and the Reverend John Phear, M.A., was at the rectory. There were three blacksmiths: Edmund Jacobs, J. Frederick Runnacles and Edmund Taylor, who was also a wheelwright. Then came four shoemakers: William Ling, Samuel Mills, John Pierpont and John F. Runnacles. And no less than twenty-six farmers, including John Fulcher, Elijah Howlett, Cornelius Nunn, Robert Plowman and Peter Kersey.

By 1879 it was different. Hamlet Watling was the master of the "Endowed School", Zephanaiah Chapman was at the 'Angel', Frederick Last a robe maker, Charles William Sutton a brewer's chemist, and Mrs James Chenery shopkeeper; but only two blacksmiths, one being Frederick Runnacles at Forward Green, and nineteen farmers, including Mrs Elizabeth Bennett.

This brings us to the wonderful little church with its wizardry of workmanship, much of which it is happy to say was created by local hands. In the thirteenth century it probably had a central tower, but even now it is cruciform, and partakes of the Early

English, Perpendicular and Decorated styles. Although quite small, it has the effect of spaciousness by reason of the clerestory windows and transepts. But its greatest claim to magnificence is in the great span of the roof of the nave. The single hammer-beam of chestnut is reputed to be one of the finest of its kind. Surely that is a great claim for any church, especially so for that of a small Suffolk village. The Stuart pulpit dates from the time of James II, and cost, £10, was undoubtedly a large sum in those days. Here also is a curious collection of four hour-glasses, a group of three registering a quarter, half and one hour. Although the poor illiterate couldn't read, they would undoubtedly have watched the sand as it fell, writhing at the length of an hour-glass long, expecially as they would have listened to the same store of wisdom more than once. But the little bit I like most of all, tribute to those marvellous builders, is to be seen in a little window of yellow glass set over the pulpit. At midday the sun shines through this on to the rood screen, shedding a soft gold light.

In the '70s restoration work was being carried out, when some wall paintings were uncovered. Fortunately for Earl Stonham, Hamlet Watling was the schoolmaster of the then recently erected school for one hundred children. He was also an antiquarian of note and recorded these, some so soon to disappear. His drawings are in the church.

The chancel has a piscina of unusual dimensions, and opposite is a sepulchre which was opened by Mr Watling in 1860. It was found to contain a Latin Prayer Book. When the restoration took place a fleur-de-lys cross was found under the floor of the south transept, and this was placed in the sepulchre. Some two-pronged forks and a knife were also found, thought to have been used by the Puritans for eating the sacramental bread.

This small village, nestling at the bottom of two hills, has a Roman origin, and is thought by some to have been Sitomajus. Its name has probably derived from the Earls of Norfolk, because the lordship of the manor was once in the possession of Thomas de Brotherton, Earl of Norfolk.

It has one more claim to a local fame, for here was the birth-place of James Bird, who was born at Deersbolt Hall, 10th November 1788. He was of puritan stock, and proud of it, commencing life at the village school. And this is what he wrote about it, as well he might:

> Born in a dear, delightful rustic spot,
> 'Mid Nature's sweetest, though secluded bowers,
> I drew my first breath in no lowly cot;
> My 'father's hall', though destitute of towers,
> Rose high o'er stately oaks, and hill and grot,
> And rich domains, and verdant meads and flowers,
> To Heaven aspiring, in its 'pride of place'.

8. BEHIND THE SCENES

There is nothing which has yet been contrived by man, by which so much happiness is produced as by a good tavern or inn.

Johnson

It is surely usual to approach an inn by the front door, but that is not always the most fascinating picture which such a place can offer. The old Dutch Masters knew that and delighted to portray the kitchens with their utensils, littered floors, and the game, fowls and fish that were about to be prepared for the feast of unlimited extent. Wordsworth once wrote this to a dairy:

> Thou unassuming common-place
> Of Nature, with that homely face,
> And yet with something of a grace
> Which love makes for thee.

He might equally have ascribed this to an inn kitchen, and a yard, such as this photograph of the back of the 'White Hart', Blythburgh, taken on 24th May 1892. It provides an interesting study.

Why did the photographer choose this aspect of the house? He must have been an artist because this is a perfect piece of composition. It was taken on the eve of Lady Day, doors and windows are fastened, the shadows not too deep and there is not a soul about. I would suggest it was high noon because of the vertical shadow under the birdcage; but I may be wrong. In any case it is a scene of antique peace, caught for all time on a few square inches of luminous paper.

This came into my possession when Rosie Mills, the smiling

daughter of the house, grew into old age. I used to spend lovely hours, sitting by her fire and talking of old times. She was so proud of the ancient inn, and of her father and mother, who ran it with such genuine hospitality. With it too, I have an unfinished water-colour sketch of the same scene, so obviously done by a master hand that one would give much to know his name. He must have returned to his studio too soon. And yet, on the other hand, if it had become a completed picture, it would not have come my way. After all, Schubert's Unfinished Symphony vies in loveliness with those of other masters' works that suggest a perfect finish.

The 'White Hart' at that time was famous, and a well-known retreat for the art world. It was kept by George Mills, who was also a farmer. True, it was on the highway to Lowestoft and Yarmouth, but the railways had reduced the traffic to a minimum. The wheels that grated by were those drawn by Suffolk Punches, interspersed with the pony carts of the old cattle dealers and the occasional gentle clip-clop of the squire's carriage. It might be of Lord and Lady Stradbroke from Henham, their own particular squire; Sir Rafe Blois from Yoxford, a considerable landowner in the locality; or Colonel Barne from Dunwich. Then, of course, there might be the lone horseman out on exercise. And the air was full of country scents and sounds that impregnated every inch and detail of life.

Perhaps one of the saddest of the sights was that of the knacker's cart, with a red sloping backboard. On this would be a pair of poor old legs ending in bright iron shoes that had ended their career. The carcass was still worth a shilling or two, hence the last journey.

But the photograph shows the backhouse where all the work was done, and which was in reality the heart of the house. One can imagine the traffic in and out, clicking over the bit of platform made from any piece of stone, brick or pebble that came to hand. In wet weather the feet would be wearing pattens, a sort of clog with a raised metal ring on the instep that lifted the wearer out of the mud and dirt. A pair of these would be hanging on the backhouse door. Sometimes it was necessary to wear them on the roads, so dirty and full of puddles were they. Pattens were the thing on washing day, and that festival is commemorated by the props that lean against the old shed in the distance. (I wonder what was in that shed in the way of what we should now call bygones?) Although folks didn't bathe themselves they were wonderful clean—because, as dear old Gilbert White reminds us, "Does not the skylark dust?"

Now comes the pump in the foreground, a real good old specimen, with an iron handle that shone like old silver and ending in a blob like a lion's tail. Pumps needed attention, hence the wooden drop front with its button so that the plumber could get at the innards. This particular specimen has a wooden trough so that the overspill can run into the soakaway and not make a mess in the yard. Also, there is a wooden bucket to catch any drips, attended by a sturdy old iron pail. Here then, was the water supply at their backdoor, one that never froze up and was free of any rate demands. And you will remember, it wasn't everybody who had a pump in their back garden, or a well either. You might have to walk a long way for a pail of water, Jack and Jill fashion.

That brings us to the brewing tubs and barrels by the gabled extension. This would almost suggest that they brewed their own beer, but I should hardly think so; perhaps they brewed some of a special variety for harvest or Christmas. The tub was known as a keeler. In it the malt was mashed and the yeast added as the liquor was baled out from the copper and left to cool to blood heat. These utensils had to be kept clean and scalded before a brew, lest the beer should be tainted.

There are two kennels, but only one is occupied, and even the dog is asleep. The back door, it must be remembered, was a rare place for gipsy callers. The shed just beyond is for the wood, or kindling, because the dark object under the clothes props is a chopping block. Life was lived the hard way, but it was no drudgery, rather something that had come down through all the years and was cheerfully followed: kindling for the fires, candles or rushlights made from the fat saved up in the kitchen, and oil lamps that shed a soft and pleasant glow. How lovely was such a parlour at eventide when "all the fading landscape sinks in night". A clear fire, a gently shaded lamp, grandmother in her chair, feet on a footstool, lace cap on her head, and a pair of steel spectacles; together with a needle hard at work. But how dark were those nights without a moon, an almost suffocating blackness to those not used to it. No wonder the black dog Old Shock or Shuck, haunted country footpaths on such a night. (An old man living not far away used to say in his own language, "I'll ha' white hogs, I'll hev no more black uns; ta mak my back-yard that black-dark, ma wife dunnaw wan tew git up i' the marnin'!")

A dove waits at the door (there are others on the roof), and a large bird is in the cage. Perchance it is a jackdaw, brought up from early youth and able to talk. It can enjoy the sunshine if not the freedom.

But of the building itself, untouched this many a year. One can almost detect a Dutch influence in the wonderful array of old red tiles, although they would have been made locally. Blythburgh faces Holland, that land of homeliness, as the crow flies. The gable-end of the house itself is definitely Dutch, and in the old days when dyking and river banks needed much attention, men of that country came here to work.

The windows are fascinating, set in the excoriated red brick. Tiny panes of old glass that resemble the horn which they re-placed, let in a little light, but were seldom opened. The whole face of it, weather-beaten, looking towards the sea and recalling lost days when greatness came to their town, ebbed and flowed and finally passed away. In those far-off days this fine old inn was the court house, where justice was dispensed, hence the splendid woodwork within in ceilings and staircase. When fires raged in the old medieval town in 1667 and again in 1696, it is good to realize this lovely old house stood firm, while the centre of the town perished.

Eastwards to the right leads to Westwood Lodge, once the home of the Hoptons—evidence of their possession is to be seen in a head of a man wearing a Tudor cap. At one time this was built into the gable-head of the old house, before it was refronted as it appears today. By degrees the house sank in importance and became a farmhouse of the Coopers, famous for sheep. At one time Mrs Catherine Cooper was the farmer. Sheep sales were then in great evidence as this notice for August 1783:

"The Westwood Lodge lambs and some others in the neighbour-hood will be offered to sale at the White Hart inn, Blythburgh, on Thursday, the 21st instant; where all gentlemen farmers who chuse

to favour me with their company will meet with a hearty welcome
from their humble servant

Rob. Sherington
Dinner at One o'clock."

Just one thing more. When the old cottage known as the Alms-
house was destroyed by fire, it was occupied by an old man whose
greatest treasure was a toilet set. A neighbour anxious to come to
the rescue of such a possession, threw it out of the window.

VIII

AND BATTLES LONG AGO

-----------------••✛••------------------

> Marching, marching, ever marching
> 'Neath the Sun-God's madd'ning glow—
> Soul-sick, weary, staggering, parching,
> Following still a phantom foe.

It is really astonishing, when you come to think of it, how the villages have contributed to the history of our island story. It was the lads of the village who marched away, too often to return no more, while it was the sons of the manors and the rectories who led them on. One has only to go into small village churches to read the records, and to note the war memorials.

Although Middleton did not produce anyone of consequence as far as is known, Theberton, the next village did. There, Squire Doughty had a son in the old army, and another an admiral, the soldier gaining a posthumous V.C. in ill-fated Gallipoli. However, it was different in the First Sikh War, because near the south porch of the old church, amongst the tumbled graves, where

> Each in his narrow cell for ever laid,
> The rude forefathers of the hamlet sleep,

is one marked by a simple headstone which can be clearly read:

> In Memory of Charles Godward of Her Majesty's
> 16th. Lancers who distinguished himself in the battles of
> Mahrajpoor, Ruddawal, Aliwal and Sobraon.
> He died at the age of 52 years, 1871.

Although it is not clear that he was born in Middleton, he was of that stock, because the Godward line went a long way back, and is a good old Suffolk name. It is said he had been apprenticed to a wig maker in London in his earlier years, but ran away to join the army and soon found himself on board one of those old sailing troopers on his way to India. Obviously he had received something of an education and been taught the art of writing. When he came home, having survived the dreadful climate and conditions, he found his way to Middleton, married a village girl who was known to all and sundry as Cousin Mary Godward, eked out a small pension with hairdressing, survived only a few years and received a wonderful funeral, being followed to his grave by local squires and gentry.

During his service in India he wrote home a quite remarkable letter, in a really beautiful hand, an eyewitness account of the battle of Aliwal, only a day or two after the event. He was then 25 years of age, and it confirms the account as given in official records. It contrasts strangely with what any private soldier could have written about an action in the First or Second World Wars, since they would have known only of what was happening immediately in front of them.

The first Sikh War, or Sutlej campaign, was brought about by the insubordination of the Sikh army, which after the death of Ranjit Singh became uncontrollable. On 11th December 1845, it crossed the Sutlej and virtually declared war on the British, who were under the command of Sir Hugh Gough.

Wearied with long marches, the British troops were enjoying a rest when the news came in that the Sikhs were advancing to battle at four o'clock in the afternoon. In the battle of the Moodkee that followed, our victory was complete against very superior forces. The next engagement, known as the battle of Ferozeshah, was against Lal Singh, who was joined later by his brother Tej Singh. This also ended in favour of the British.

Now came Aliwal, fought under the command of Sir Harry Smith, who advanced from Ludhiana to attack the Sikh left, near the village of Aliwal. This was a key position, where a brilliant charge by the 16th Lancers broke up the Sikh square. The enemy fled in confusion losing sixty-seven guns.

Sobraon, fought on 10th February, concluded the First Sikh War. Gough attacked the enemy who occupied a strongly entrenched position in the bend of the Sutlej. The advance of the first brigade was not immediately successful, but the second brigade carried the entrenchments. The cavalry then charged down the Sikh lines from right to left and completed the victory, the enemy suffering terrible carnage. After the battle the British advanced to Lahore, where the treaty was signed on 11th March. So Aliwal was not the end of Private Godward's war, but he was dead right in his reckoning of the next engagement, as evidenced by his letter.

Of the letter itself the address is of great interest. The position in the camp is definitely stated, so unlike information kept with such secrecy in World War I. Then a large '2' on the outer wrapper seems to give it a modern flavour, as if it were mixed up with second-class mail. The signature, or franking, of the commanding officer would almost suggest censoring. But what a flutter of excitement the letter must have caused in quiet Middleton Street, when it arrived "via Southampton". The deciphered contents follow, but the folded line proved impossible. This has been guessed at, although it has little or no effect on the tale that is told.

It might be mentioned in passing that the regiment was founded in 1759 and the 16th Light Dragoons were converted into Lancers in 1816. They were at Waterloo. They arrived in India in 1825 and left in 1846.

From No. 1233 Chas. Godward Pt. H.M. 16th Lancers.

To S. Clark

Middleton,

Via Southampton.   Near Yoxford,

J. H.   Suffolk England.

Commanding H.M. 16th., Lancers.

Camp Left Bank of the River

Sutlej, Ist. Feby, 1846.

My Dear Uncle.

It is one of the proudest moments of my life to be able and here to take my pen in hand to pen these few lines to you after this long silence in extenuation of which I can say nothing, it is neglect and it is not. I certainly should have wrote had we been more settled, for to tell you the truth of late affairs have been in such confusion that I did not like writing as one time we were coming home and at others we were going into the field. The former we made sure of, and the latter although little expected by me and many more, as come true, however, to cut the subject short I through myself intirely on your kindness for forgiveness and proceed at once to our frequent movements. You will doubtless long before this comes to hear or read in the English newspapers of the threatened invasion of India by the Lehorans, one of the strongest powers in India, and had actually marched into British India with that intention. Our government immediately assembled an Army to oppose them, in which we were embodied, we joined Head Quarters in the beginning of last month (Jany). On the 19th. of last month the Division, what the 16th. Lancers belonged to, moved from the main body to rout a large body of the enemy who had assembled within four marches of ours. On the 21st. we came up with them, but in consequence of marching all night we could not engage with them, so had to make a good retreat, which we did in a masterly style, recruited in a few days and again moved to attack them on the morning of the 28th. and after a long and well contested battle on both sides, we gained a complete victory over them, captured all their guns, stores, ammunition and tentage and drove them over and into the river, with a very severe loss, and but a trifling loss on our part. My own regiment I regret to say suffered most, our loss in killed and wounded amounted to 140. Many of the wounded will I think never join the ranks again, but I hope they may, however myself and many more escaped I know not. Our regiment charged and broke up two infantry squares and captured several guns, and the more I think of the affair, the more it surprises me to think how we escaped. I hope sincerely that in the next engagement I may come out as safe as this, without a scratch. We expect the final engagement will take place on the 8th. or 10th. of this month, but I will if possible write to you by the first mail that leaves after it. This last engagement was the second achieved. In the two we have taken two hundred brass guns, all splendidly mounted and in excellent order. That is all the news I can send you this mail and am sorry I cannot enter into more details, but time does not admit of it, but when all is over I will endeavour to write you more particulars, but most likely you will see them in the English newspapers before. I must now conclude with my kind remembrances to all friends at home, tell them I am quite well, and all the news I send, so with my love to you from

Your
Affectionate and Dutiful
Nephew
Chas. Godward.

And remember these battles were fought in red coats under a scorching sun. While the wounded if they fell into the hands of the surgeons had but a slender hope of survival.

If the village of Middleton is connected with the First Sikh War, Old Felixstowe parish church has a connection with the battle of Waterloo in no uncertain manner, because in the nave, just westwards of the south door is an oval tablet that has been removed from the old chancel, when the new chancel and transepts were built. It reads: "In this Chancel lie interred the remains of Adam Wood Esq of the Independent Company of Invalids at Landguard Fort, who died June 10, 1773; and of Frances, his relict, who died January 3, 1822, aged 85. This Tablet is erected as a mark of filial affection by Sir George Adam Wood, K.C.B. and K.M.T. Major Genl Sir G. A. Wood, K.C.H. died 22nd. April 1831. Aged 62, buried at Paddington."

Now Adam Wood Esq. was the father of a most distinguished soldier who was in sole charge of the artillery on that immortal morning of 18th June 1815 when the Battle of Waterloo was fought and won. His career is given in brief in the *Dictionary of National Biography*, thus: "Sir George Adam Wood (1767–1831), major general Royal Artillery: studied at Woolwich; second lieutenant, 1808: major general 1825; served in Flanders, 1793–5, West Indies, 1795–7, Mediterranean, 1806–8, Portugal, 1808–9, and Walcherin, 1809; knighted 1812; in Holland and Flanders, 1813–14; commanded whole of artillery in Waterloo Campaign, 1815, and British artillery in army of occupation in France, 1819; governor of Carlisle, 1825."

It is perhaps not surprising that books are still being written about the famous battle and Wellington, "He that won a hundred fights nor ever lost an English gun." One published not long ago, entitled *A Near Run Thing*, is supposed to have been Wellington's version of the affair. And from all accounts it was. Now another has appeared, written by a distant descendant of Wellington's wife and entitled *Wellington: The Years of the Sword*. Not yet have the disparagers arisen to debunk the victor, but it is certain they will soon have to get to work, particularly if they run out of subject matter.

A good deal of legend has had to be discarded, such as, for instance, the view that Waterloo was won on the playing fields of Eton. Or that other little dialogue with one of the Pagets, who said, "By Gad, Sir, I have just lost my leg!" To which Wellington is supposed to have replied, "By Gad, Sir, so you have!" Or even,

"Up Guards and at 'em!" But it remains true that Wellington delegated his responsibilities to no one, and if he did think his men were the scum of the earth, he saw that they were well fed.

Coming back to Sir George Adam Wood, who was as much in the thick of it, I read this in *A Near Run Thing*: " 'Damn it, Mercer,' a voice said, 'you have hot work of it here.' Sir George Adam Wood, the veteran Commander of artillery, appeared through the smoke and shell fire. He was blinking, Mercer observed, as a man does when he is facing a gale of wind. 'Yes, sir, pretty hot,' Mercer said with soldierly modesty and began to give the general an account of what had happened."

Waterloo was a full-dress occasion, in which those old cannons played such a large part. They belched forth smoke to such an extent that the battlefield was almost in a fog, but the carnage was awful. It was they and the cavalry that carried the day and ushered in the Long Peace that extended from 1816 to 1852.

Felixstowe parish church can claim two other military heroes. A typical Victorian memorial of marble and granite is to be found in the churchyard, erected to the memory of Sir John Spencer Login by his ward, the Maharajah Duleep Singh. True he only lived in Felixstowe a few months, but he left his bones there. He had seen service in the Afghan and Sikh Wars, as also in the Mutiny, so he could have linked hands with the private in the 16th Lancers. He was a surgeon at the Residency, Lucknow.

Then comes Field-Marshal Viscount Allenby of Megiddo and of Felixstowe in the county of Suffolk. Though not born in the village, he spent his early years there. His memorial was unveiled in the parish church just fifty years after the liberation of Jerusalem, but his ashes are in Westminster Abbey.

And to end, a Sir Thomas Gooch of Benacre Park was the first person to suggest to the Government the plan of raising provincial corps of yeomanry cavalry throughout the kingdom. His proposal was made in December 1799 and soon after adopted generally in Great Britain and Ireland. Sir Thomas bore the rank of first lieutenant under Lord Rous in the first troop of the Suffolk yeomanry to be organized in the county.

When a collection was being made in Suffolk villages for sufferers in the Boer War, an old couple gave a whole shilling (wages were then about 10s. a week). Asked by the lady collector if they could really spare it, the reply came, "Yes, ma'am, my husband wishes to do it." Then the husband came forward. "My father, ma'am was wounded at the battle of Waterloo, and my mother and two children had to go into the 'House'." Such was a country memory gilded by a fine pride.

CHAPTER IX

VILLAGE TIME PIECES

····❧····

What is a church? Our honest sexton tells,
'Tis a tall building, with a tower and bells.
Go; of my Sexton seek. Whose days are sped?
What! he himself!—and is old Dubble dead?
His eightieth year he reached, still undecay'd
And rectors five to one close vault convey'd;
But he is gone; his care and skill I lose
And gain a mournful subject to my Muse.
Crabbe.

I wonder what would be said today if the papers or television got hold of the news that a man had kept his job for seventy years, and had not been absent once in fifty years? There would be screaming headlines, photographers would be falling over themselves to get a picture and the newsmen a story. Such was the record of William Pipe of Theberton, a delightful village not far from the sea of the Suffolk coast, the last of its parish clerks.

He became parish clerk in 1823, leading the singing in succession to his father, and held office until death. William had a fine musical voice, and was skilled in music and bell ringing. Like his father before him, he carried on the trade of a shoemaker, and with many other avocations was a farmer in a small way, hiring some scattered fields, doing most of the work himself—even to his own harvest the last year of his life, at the age of 89. A tall thin man with a fine head, he once walked to Ipswich on business, intending to come back in the old Blue Coach as far as Saxmundham. The coach overtook him soon after he left Ipswich, but he let it pass and thus saved the fare. He was then in middle age and had walked 54 miles without fatigue. He died in 1892 and was buried near his father in the old churchyard.

William Pipe had been chief citizen and leader for seventy years.

John Pipe had been leader and conductor of the company of singers (before choirs). He died in 1823, having served as clerk and sexton for more than twenty-five years. In 1820 he tolled the bell for the funeral of King George III. His trade of shoemaker for a small village was extensive, employing some five or six journeymen. He appears to have kept a school also, which might even have been held in the church porch, or as Goldsmith has it:

> Beside yon straggling fence that skirts the way
> With blossom'd furze unprofitably gay—
> There, in his noisy mansion, skill'd to rule,
> The village master taught his little school.

Thus father and son together held the sacred office for nearly a century.

Of William's record a charming account was written many years ago by a daughter of the hall under the pen-name of 'Amyas Revett'—presumably she was Katherine Doughty, author of *The Betts of Wortham*.

"Went for a drive to see Mrs Pipe's baby." This is an entry in my grandmother's diary. It is followed soon by another entry— "Went to Town in the Shannon coach." Now the Shannon coach has long since made its last journey: the baby is an elderly man; but the baby's father is only lately dead.

When that journal was written he had already been married sixteen years, and for twenty-one years had been parish clerk, sexton and schoolmaster in our little east country village.

[Miss Doughty goes on:] There have been many changes during seventy years, and when first appointed in succession to his father, he was doubtless a far greater man than he was at his death. Few of his class then could read, and he was truly the voice of the people, as he led them through prayer and psalm, speaking slowly, and in the Suffolk dialect which they all could follow. Now the responses are said by the choir, but there are a few old people, survivors of those unlettered days, who stand with vacant eyes and bookless hands, lost without a guiding voice they had learned so well to understand.

"The church will never feel itself without him", they say, and it certainly does not look itself. He made a picture sitting in his carved seat below the reading desk, a larger prayer book open before him, and the light from a south window falling on his snowy hair and lion-like face, revered with age. When he stood he was taller than most of the congregation, and leaned forward his face lighted with pleasure, as his musical old voice started the chants and hymns.

It is sad to think how few of his friends are left to remember even fifty years ago; none can remember a time when he was not clerk; he had but one contemporary—an old woman—and she outlived him by a few days. Yet though the people are changed, the village remains nearly as it was that distant day when his mother carried him up to the quaint reed-thatched church to be christened.

The interior of the church has been altered even since the days of my grandmother. The high pews are gone, a vestry has been built out from the north door hiding a beautiful Norman arch, and the singing gallery has vanished. In it young Pipe used to lead the "musick" of flutes and fiddles, ere he moved down to sit among the schoolboys, upon whose heads he wielded the actual staff of authority. The pulpit hath, saith tradition, been moved so often that an old churchwarden suggested that it should be furnished with wheels, so that the "reverends" could place it where they pleased, without further expense to the parish. . . .

Of course they made enemies, and many an envious word has passed about their pride. "So proud that they would shake the tablecloth out in the garden, even if they had had no dinner." The wife was truly frugal, going to bed, most of the year with the sun to save her candles, and it was said that they were miserly; but yet, when in their old age their hopes were raised by an advertisement, promising a legacy of a hundred punds to persons of their name, their first thought was to put a clock in the church tower. Of course they never got the money, and she regretted the clock even more than he did. Mahala Nunn was her maiden name and when she was married, she must have been a beautiful girl. She was pretty even when I knew her, a gentle, quaintly sentimental old dame, devoted to her garden, with its double row of flowers on each side of the path. Some were in bloom at every season of the year. The earliest crocuses, snowdrops, and violets would be there in spring; then would come tulips, hyacinths, anemones, and double daisies. Then a crowd of roses, larkspurs, Jacob's ladder, and pansies; then tall lilies; then sweet-williams, poppies, china asters, and more roses, till her chrysanthemums, the pride of her heart, made an avenue of glory in the autumn. It was a good sight to see the old couple together; and their children long ago out in the world and far away, they were everything to each other; he tending her flowers and daily bringing her in a fresh nosegay; she very proud of him, and never failing to show strangers the clock which the parish had given him on his jubilee of clerkship, and the inscription recording the fact, that never once in all those years had he missed any sacred services. And in those services she took the greatest interest, grieving much at any falling off of the congregation. "Oh, we do fare right undressed, we fare whooly naked on Sundays", was her lament, when a family which filled three pews left the village.

She died five years before her husband, after sixty-one years of married life, and the old man's grief was a bitter sight to see.

He was a farmer among his other avocations, getting in his own harvest at the age of eighty nine, and spraining his back by carrying too heavy a ladder. He had one red cow, which could never be kept within bounds, jumping any fence, and always thin and bony with hard exercise. The girls in the village held it in awe, for it was as he expressed it, "very playful with young females."

Opposite the forge stands the inn. It used to be a sort of club for the farmers to meet and smoke together, but one day the young "min" from the hamlet stormed it, and being armed with ground ashes, drove their betters out with great discomfiture, since then it has not been so popular with them. Still, here was held the annual tithe dinner, at which old Pipe never once failed to give a toast and song. There was no nonsense about the old man, no official hypocrisy. He could be merry and jovial with the best. He must have had a paternal feeling for the whole village; the old men he had taught as boys, he had seen their parents baptised and married, and he had dug the graves of more than two generations. Sunday was the day to see him in his glory; he would stand watch in hand, timing his changes as the congregation came in, for he was a prince among bell-ringers.

(Thro' Grandsires and Triples with pleasure men range
Till Death calls the Bob, and brings on the last change).

But, alas! there came a Sunday when old Pipe could not come to church, and he was "very sorry to leave the clergyman by himself, for he is a young gentleman." And there came another, when watching with a gleam of sunlight, which had always lighted up his grand old face, pass over his empty seat and then suddenly fade into chill darkness, the writer wondered whether his spirit had gone with it, for it was known his hours were numbered.

Alone, save for a hired housekeeper and one son, who came too late for recognition, our old friend passed away; and of his supposed hoards were found none, though his assembled family searched long for them.

The village is a different place; the church seems empty; the bright garden is a patch of brown earth; and the stranger, a Londoner, inhabits the old house.

There is a new mound beside Mahala Pipe's grave; some day the village will put a headstone to it.

The headstone near his father's was duly erected, inscribed: "This stone has been erected to his memory by his friends and fellow parishioners as a mark of respect for his worth." He was 90 and died in 1892.

I have quoted from this article because it was written by an eyewitness of such an old established office, the last to hold it. Moreover it is written in such a charming manner by one who was proud to call Suffolk her home after many generations. It was her niece who modelled those marvellous little coloured birds that gained for our country such large numbers of dollars in the Second World War. But the record was nothing out of the way in old Suffolk, particularly amongst sextons and parish clerks. What a wonderful race they were, prominent figures in the village community, sometimes lamenting the fact that no one died in the parish, but on the job when anyone did:

> Forty-eight years strange to tell,
> He bore the bier and toll'd the bell,
> And faithfully discharged his trust
> In earth to earth, and dust to dust.

In so many cases the sexton could neither read nor write, but that was no matter of consequence. When one of the parsons said he would have to take the matter in hand, the reply was: "Whoi sur, if I must read jist like a yeow, thare 'ont be no difference atween us." Incidentally, he was the one who sometimes got overheated when working. But realizing his labours were on consecrated ground, respected the situation and rushed out into the road to give expression to his feelings.

A good story was related by W. Mowbray Donne about a female clerk. The clergyman gave out the Psalms for the sixteenth day of the month. The clerk looked up to him from her box below the reading desk and said, "the seventeenth." The clergyman, rather nettled, rejoined, "The sixteenth." "Well," said the lady, "I'm a gooin' to read the seventeenth." The clergyman succumbed to his clerk's choice. Afterwards, he naturally called her to book, when she replied, "Thass like this here, I ha' to git up my Psalms in the week an' I made a mistake. I know you could read 'em for either day, but yew see, I cudn't."

Neither, of course, were they overpaid, sexton or clerk, although some of them made up their income on a bit of smuggling, especially the sextons. However, that might have been said of some of the parsons. No wonder the latter held on until death, for many Suffolk livings were fat indeed. Yet some of these incumbents were as their name implied, parsimonious. Not forgetting the tale told by A. J. Swinburne, Her Majesty's Schools Inspector for Suffolk in the days of Queen Victoria.

He spent a night at a country rectory when five adults sat down to dine off a pigeon. He was asked to carve and would he give the first helping to a mother-in-law upstairs. Believe it or not, the old bird didn't run to a second helping. Let's hope they fared better in the kitchen behind the green baize doors.

The classic portrait of a parish clerk was painted by Thomas Gainsborough—and he looks quite distinguished. In some cases they bore high-sounding local names. For example, at Spexhall in 1879, the lord of the manor was Sir Edward C. Kerrison, Baronet, and the parish clerk was George Kerrison. The question is, did the latter have to pull his forelock to the former?

Then at Tattingstone in the churchyard is a memorial to a William Talmash, who departed this life the 22nd July 1804, aged 83 years. It concludes: "An honest man's the noblest work of God." He was parish clerk for nearly fifty years and derived, it is said, from the younger son of Nicholas Talmash, who was thought to have been the son of the Hon. Captain Talmash or Tollemache (died 1691), who was the youngest son of Sir Lionel Tollemache and his wife, Elizabeth, Countess of Dysart. How a member of so well known a Suffolk family became the parish clerk, tradition says happened thus. Captain Tollemache, while fighting a duel is said to have killed his opponent. Fearing the result of his action, the report was spread abroad that he had fled the country, but in reality he remained at Helmingham Hall for the rest of his life. He contracted a marriage with a farmer's daughter and from that union sprang a son, Nicholas, who in turn married and had a son William, later in life to be the clerk at Tattingstone. Therefore he could claim to be a member of the family of whom the couplet tells:

> When William the Conqueror reigned with great fame,
> Bentley was my seat and Tollemache was my name.

The sextons, of course, were a race apart, and part of their job was to dig. And the strange thing was—yet not so strange—they were always coming across something. I like the account of one Henry Naylor, who dug up a load of old glass at Icklingham All Saints, "sufficient to fill a peck measure." He was whooly stammed at the old stuff and the fuss they made about it. But there, some learned old parson had it replaced in the church windows, where it lets in a golden light to this very day.

Or the tale about the old sexton at Wenhaston, when the whitewashed boards that had filled the tympanum of the chancel arch were thrown out into the churchyard at a restoration that was in progress. He was walking the next morning to perform his duties, when he suddenly spied a lot of old faces looking up at him, and was so taken aback that he ran off home as fast as his legs would carry him. The storm in the night had washed off the covering and revealed the marvellous painting of the Doom that was underneath and which is such a treasured survival to this day.

Then too, the sextons were often bellringers, and in some Suffolk belfries their place at the ropes is denoted by badges of office, such as at Gislingham. On the ringers' board, number one bell is pictured with a spade and coffin. At Pettaugh a tablet in the west wall records a gift to the parish, 8th March 1842, of a cottage, garden and 2 acres of land, the rent of which was to go to the sexton's wages, church repairs and parish expenses.

I suppose one of the best epitaphs to a sexton ever made, was to be found in the belfry of Hadleigh church, now long since vanished:

> See, Ringers read, John Hills lies here
> Our Sexton, eight and fifty years.
> The Steeple, which he kept, him keeps,
> Lo! under the great bell he sleeps.
> Ring on, no noyse him wakes, untill
> Christ's trumpet every grave unfill.
> Sepultus est Mar. 27 1625.

Upon the same wall to the east was this addition:

> The Church, the Clock, each Bell
> He tended wonderous well.
> The proverb is not dead
> What his due care then bred,
> As sure as Key and Lock
> As true as Hadleigh Clock.

It appears that John Hills was buried 7th March 1626, and that a "Robt Hyll, sexton of the church of Hadleigh", whose burial is recorded in the register for 1568, was probably his father. The latter is mentioned in the churchwarden's account book for 1561: "payd for nayle which Hyll occupied for the bell, Id."

It was said that those old untutored clerks had a very shrewd judgement of the incumbents they served. When banns were called, they were known in old Suffolk as sybrits. Forby writes: "It is one of Sir Thomas Browne's words, and in full use at this day." The word was derived from 'sib', said to mean akin; and to imply, that by banns the parties have a right to become akin, that is sib-right. I must say I rather like the way in which some couples approached the matter, such as: "Mr Watson, you may tell the clergyman to talk about William Nash and Elizabeth Clements."

To return to William Pipe, he was not only a lover of his job, but also of his ancient church of Norman origin. The photograph (facing page 176) shows him standing at the south porch, with caressing hands on the old fabric. It has one of those round towers of uncertain age, with an octagon top of later date. I should also like to tell you that the old shrine was not altogether innocent of a bit of smuggling, when they hid a few kegs under the drape of the holy table.

In process of time, both offices of sexton and clerk got mixed up together. Now both have passed away, to lead the singing of mis-pronounced Psalms no more for ever.

> God save the King! Will no man say, amen?
> Am I both priest and clerk? Well then, amen!

CHAPTER X

THE LIFEBOAT THAT WENT TO CHURCH

····❧····

The first one in the lifeboat, and who so brave as he?
His voice was heard above the storm, above the howling sea;
What could excel that noble heart amid the billow's strife,
As with his brave and daring crew they risked each precious life.

The Suffolk and Norfolk coast in the days of sail were dreadful
for wrecks. A terrible storm 'in the memory of man' occurred at
Lowestoft on the 18th December 1770.

It began about one o'clock in the morning and continued with
increasing violence till five, when the wind suddenly changed
from the south-east to the north-west. Anchors and cables proved
too feeble a security for the ships, which instantly parting from them,
and running on board each other, produced a confusion neither to
be described nor conceived; not a few immediately foundered,
others were dismantled, and none escaped unhurt. At day-light . . .
no less than eighteen ships were on the sand . . . and many others
were seen to sink . . . the unhappy men . . . betook themselves to the
masts and rigging; these constantly breaking, eight or ten were not
infrequently seen to perish at a time . . . fifteen only . . . were
taken off one wreck. . . . It is impossible to collect how many lives
or ships were lost. Twenty-five or thirty ships, and two hundred
men, do not seem to be an exaggerated account.

Ruskin once said he considered one of the finest sea pieces ever
conceived was Dickens' description of a great storm at Yarmouth,
as told in *David Copperfield*:

"What is the matter?" I cried.
"A wreck! Close by!"
"A schooner from Spain or Portugal, laden with fruit and wine.
Make haste, sir, if you want to see her!"

There was a bell on board; and as the ship rolled and dashed, like a desperate creature driven mad, now showing us the whole sweep of her deck, as she turned on her beam ends towards the shore, now nothing but her keel, as she sprung wildly over and turned towards the sea, the bell rang; and its sound, the knell of those unhappy men, was borne towards us on the wind. Again we lost her and again she rose. Two men were gone. The agony on shore increased. Men groaned and clasped their hands; women shrieked and turned away their faces. Some ran wildly up and down along the beach, crying for help where no help could be. . . .

Another cry arose on shore; and looking to the wreck, we saw the cruel sail, with blow on blow, beat off the lower of the two men and fly up in triumph round the active figure left alone upon the mast.

It was not surprising that Yarmouth churchyard contained many memorials of shipwrecks in the days of Nall the local historian and recorder of dialect. The following come from his volume:

Boast not of tomorrow, for thou knowest not what a day may bring forth.

In memory of
John Cutter ⎫ ⎧ 29 ⎫
Thomas Foster ⎬ aged ⎨ 29 ⎬ Years.
Richard Barrett ⎭ ⎩ 19 ⎭

late belonging to His Majesty's sloop, the Fly, who were drowned on coming for the beach, the 15th. day of February, 1780:

When the brave tar who furls aloft the sail,
Escapes from peril and survives the gale,
How hard his fate, a thousand dangers past,
When near the friendly land to breathe his last—
Tho' rescued oft' from threat'ning seas, one wave
Upsets the boat and sends him to his grave.
Stranger! should chance direct thy footsteps here,
Cans't thou refrain to shed a gen'rous tear!
Cans't thou, now Britain on her sons must call,
Without emotion see one sailor fall.
Parading armies still may awe the land,
But England's safety on her fleet depends.

And this:

To a Sailor

Though Boreas blow, and Neptune's waves
Have toss'd me to and fro;
By God's decree, you plainly see
I'm harbour'd here below:

Where I must at anchor lie,
With many of our fleet:
But once again we shall set sail,
Our Admiral Christ to meet.

This called forth a footnote that rather intrigues me: "This appears on an older stone at Lowestoft, also at Ware. In most seaside churchyards, it furnishes the theme for numberless variations, and with 'afflictions sore', 'farewell vain world', 'a loving husband and a friend sincere' forms the mouldy stock in trade of the parish clerk and gravestone cutter." I should very much question the parish clerk's ability to provide these distiches, neither has the source of their inspiration ever been discovered.

To the memory of David Bartleman, master of the brig Alexander and Margaret, of North Shields, who, on the 31st. January, 1781, on the Norfolk coast with only three three-pounders and ten men and boys, nobly defended himself against a cutter carrying eighteen four-pounders and upwards of a hundred men, commanded by the notorious English pirate, Fall, and fairly beat him off. Two hours after, the enemy came down upon him again; when totally dismasted, his mate, Daniel MacAuly, expiring with the loss of blood, and himself dangerously wounded, he was obliged to strike and ransom. He brought his shattered vessel into Yarmouth with more than the honours of a conqueror, and died here in consequence of his wounds on the 14th. of February following, in the twenty-fifth year of his age. To commemorate the gallantry of his son, the bravery of his faithful men, and at the same time mark the infamy of a savage pirate, his afflicted father, Alexander Bartleman, has ordered this stone to be erected over his honourable grave.

'Twas great!
His foe though strong was infamous;
The foe of human kind!
A manly indignation fir'd his breast.
Thank God! My son has done his duty.

Here rest the remains of George Pandall, a native of Rhodes, who died in Yarmouth, 8th January 1818, aged 32 years:

> Early he left his native shore,
>   O'er many lands to roam,
> And entered to return no more
>   A foreign master's home.
> The parents, friends that lov'd him most,
>   Caught not his latest breath,
> But pity fill'd affection's post,
>   And smooth'd his bed of death.
> What recks it where his ashes bide,
>   He who his soul receiv'd,
> Enquires not where the wanderer died,
>   But how the Christian liv'd?

Coast erosion has been very heavy and particularly so at Pakefield near Lowestoft. In the old Ship Inn, now no more, was a rough painting showing some shipwrecked men being hauled ashore by Peek, a well known lugger skipper, and under it these lines:

> She strikes the sand, she parts the deck,
> The crew now floats upon the wreck,
> But safe from harm God guards the strand
> And keeps his Roaring Boys at hand.

Next to this was a painting of a black pyramidal tombstone inscribed:

> To the memory of Robert Peek and his Crew,
> Drowned October 30th. 1836. Memento Mori.

This brings us to the story of the Suffolk lifeboats, which is an immortal epic with names that should be inscribed in gold: such as Alfred Hook and Jack Swan of Lowestoft; Ben Herrington of Southwold; James Cable, whose grandfather and father were both drowned; Joshua Chard of Aldeburgh and Sizewell; and, not least, Dix of Dunwich. Nothing can tarnish their record, or ignore their entire disregard for personal safety. We can only dimly realize what it was to put to sea in a cockle shell, such as the boat illustrated, in the face of a raging force. If one can but stand on the shore when the water, in all its power, is running mountains high, then one can begin to wonder at the calculated bravery with which they found a watery grave.

It appears that Lowestoft had one of the first lifeboats in Suffolk. Suckling in his *History*, states that a Mr Robert Sparrow of Worlingham Hall founded a Lifeboat Society at Lowestoft on 6th September, 1800, and that a lifeboat was built the next year at a cost of £105. Another boat built at the same time was stationed at Woodbridge Haven. Both boats were built by Henry Greathead of Shields.

Dunwich, the old capital city of East Anglia, lying close to Southwold and about a wave's length from Sizewall, had only three lifeboats to its story. The station was founded in 1873, with a lifeboat house on the beach, and it continued until 1903, when the last boat had to be withdrawn.

In December 1895, when Isaac Dix retired as coxswain, owing to age, he was presented with a certificate of service and a purse of gold from the Royal National Lifeboat Institution, in recognition of his eighteen years' service. This was at a meeting held in the schoolroom when the crew attended in their lifebelts and scarlet stocking-caps. The meeting was presided over by Mr E. Lingwood, a local artist and honorary secretary of the Lifeboat Institution, and the presentation was made by Lady Constance Barne. It appeared that when the station was first established, Edward Brown was appointed at the head and Isaac Dix as second coxswain, becoming chief in 1877. Since then the lifeboat had been called out for service eight times, and had been instrumental in saving twenty-eight lives and assisting to save one vessel.

Mr Lingwood read the minutes from the book, recounting how, on the night of the 20th December 1886, when three vessels were in distress off the coast, the Dunwich lifeboat, in charge of Mr Dix, went to the rescue of the crew of the *Day Star* of Ipswich, and saved the mate, Henry Goodchild, from the rigging, where he was helpless through cold and exposure. The Southwold boat saved four men from the same vessel, the cook, John Catchpole, however, being unfortunately drowned. The seas were so heavy at the time that the coxswain of the Southwold boat was washed overboard, but afterwards rescued. The minute concluded (referring to the Dunwich boat): "The boat behaved admirably, and the crew showed great pluck."

The members of the lifeboat crew, together with the local coastguards, were afterwards entertained to a substantial dinner at the little inn—then named the 'Barne Arms', now the 'Ship'. Presumably the crew first removed their lifebelts and caps.

Our photograph (facing page 177) shows the first Dunwich lifeboat, named the *John Keble* after the author of the *Christian Year*. It was given and maintained by his family. It was drawn by horses to church to be blessed on 9th October 1873, and the picture was evidently taken on this auspicious occasion. It shows a boat of the then known Norfolk and Suffolk type, with a belt of cork round her outside below the gunwale. They were self-righting boats, but were not at all popular, although they were in service for many years.

This photograph must be somewhat unique, taken at such an early period. It is also a tribute to a skilled modern photographer who has rescued it from utter oblivion. The crew of fourteen, all village lads, look the way we always imagine lifeboatmen to have been. They are period pieces every one, as fearless as a stormy coast station could produce. The bystanders are equally interesting. But the wooden undercarriage, the huge wheels of which must have been made by a local wheelwright, mellowed by sea-water, appear as though cut from a loaf of brown bread. According to hearsay, there was a launching after the christening and one of the crew jumped overboard and swam ashore.

It might be mentioned that, although we associate John Keble with the rustic retreat of Hursley, he was of Suffolk extraction. His forbears figure in the history of Halesworth, where a James Keble, by will dated 27th January 1650, left the trustees a pightle, that the rent therefrom should be distributed in bread to the poor before Christmas. Also apparently the same man in 1652 left lands in Holton, half the revenue to be used for widows, the other half to bind out poor children as apprentices.

When Richard Whately, who became Archbishop of Dublin, was rector of Halesworth, Keble, who was a friend, went to see him with the manuscript of the *Christian Year* in his pocket. Whately advised publication.

Back to our lifeboat, the *John Keble* seems to have accomplished little in the way of rescue. She was the one, however, that rescued the mate of the *Day Star*, as mentioned above.

The second boat was the *Ann Ferguson*, a rather larger vessel, which lasted seven years. She was launched five times and saved twenty lives. One of the barques was the *Flora of Oland*, sunk on the Sizewell Bank on 3rd November 1888. The wind was strong at east-south-east and, the sea being heavy, one of the crew was washed overboard but rescued. The coxswain Isaac Dix beached the boat at Sizewell. The nameboard of the *Flora* can be seen to this day over the entrance to the tea rooms in the lane leading to the sea.

The *Lily Bird* replaced the *Ann Ferguson* in 1894, but was never used. She was removed in 1903, and Dunwich ceased to be a lifeboat station. The fact remains, those brave men would have answered the call if one had arisen.

Now comes a recipe from a little parchment-covered book, dating from 1847, supposed to have come from Dunwich. In reality it looks to me more like a tally account for barge loads of grain from vessels like *Juniper*, *Kingston*, *Helen and Sophia*, *Industry*, *Brothers*, *Vixen* and *Mariah*. It is given as written:

Resat for Rumatism. $\frac{1}{4}$ Pint Spirits Turpentine. Pint $\frac{1}{4}$ WW Vinegar. I New Laid Egg.

Resat for the Rheumatism.
1 Pennyworth of Hartshorn
1 do of oil of Swallow.
1 do of oil of St. John.
1 do of oil of Almonds
1 do of oil of Buck.
1 do of Sweet Oil.
2 Drams of Hydrat of Potash.

Nall, writing in 1866, devotes a page or two to the beachmen of this part of the coast, with especial reference to Yarmouth. Their patrol extended from the water's edge at Pakefield northwards nearly to Cromer, and corresponded to the dangerous navigation known as the Yarmouth Roads. Along this highway hundreds of ships passed daily on their way to and from the Tyne and Thames, the majority being colliers and coasters, "numbers of which are old, crazy, and indifferently found". (Defoe described the Pakefield gat as the terror of sailors, especially the Pightle, a dangerous cul-de-sac between the Scroby and Cross Sands.)

These old beachmen, who looked like the P.B.I. of yesterday, were reputed to be governed by the lowest motives, and then suddenly graded as the greatest heroes. They were recruited principally from the ranks of the herring fishermen. In the intervals between the fishing seasons, whilst the green men or country hands returned to the fields, they had to earn their livelihood with all kinds of jobs. They were divided into companies, such as the Holkham, Standard, Young, Diamond, Roberts', Star and Denney's Companies, mustering in the winter time, when the rands were full, about 180 men. Each company had a look-out furnished with telescopes, and a warehouse, or hut, for the store. They manned the local boats, clinker built, known as beach yawls—a model of one can be seen in Southwold church. Attached to their shed each company had a sitting room called a 'court'. "Here they would sit and braid trawl nets, long-shore nets, make and mend ballast bags, cut out linen pegs, play draughts, read and smoke, and keep watch by turns at night." They also fished in the roads, fetched masters of ships ashore or put them on board, put off the pilots, swept for anchors lost in the roads, or took off anchors, spars etc. to vessels needing them.

Nall goes on:

There are several popular errors current regarding the beachmen — "that they are a class apart, intermarrying among themselves, have only a few names among them, and are chiefly distinguished by nicknames." Their occupation knits them into small companies, predisposed by rival interests to look askance at those members of their own class on the beach with whom they do not usually act in concert, and this feeling is carried as far, that, as a rule, they never enter each others 'courts', even for religious or benevolent purposes. There is nothing, but the nature of their calling confining them to a strip of the beach, to keep them apart from the community. As the fishing comes round they join in it, looking down perhaps on the countrymen, as they call the capstan hands. Those who live in the fishing villages which line the coast marry naturally amongst each other. That there is a tendency to form a caste is disproved by the fact that there is an abundance of names in their ranks. Amongst the 180 beachmen at Yarmouth there are upwards of sixty different names. Nicknames were formerly the rule, but are now the exception, and are almost confined to the epithets the rival companies

10

have conferred on each other of "young uns", "strong uns", "wriggle bums", "silver spoons", etc.

The Yarmouth Life Boat is entrusted to the care of the beachmen, each company taking charge of her one year, and is usually worked by the two companies which are accustomed to act together.

Admission into the ranks of the Yarmouth beachmen is not very easy. At Lowestoft, where no difficulty is made, they are more numerous, there being upwards of 200, consisting chiefly of the men who work the half-and-half boats in the fishing. At Caistor there are 40 beachmen; at California, two miles further north, 30. Newport, in Hemsby parish, has 14; Winterton has two companies, mustering 60 hands. At the last village they consist of a few large families, the Danish patronymic of George being common, and nicknames in consequence rife. Almost all the beachmen in these villages are either masters or mates of herring boats.

The first lifeboat at Lowestoft was the *Francis Ann*, presented to the town in 1809. Early in the nineteenth century there were three beach companies still in existence: the Old Company of Lowestoft Beachmen, the Young Company and the North Roads Company. Each had its shed on the North Beach and each its yawl, and each possessed a look-out of its own. The complaint was that the steam tugs had usurped their chances of a livelihood, but had left them the manning of the lifeboats. Their old sheds were adorned with figure-heads and the nameboards of the wrecks they had sought to help.

An epic story of one Yarmouth beachman is told of Samuel Brock, who on the night of 6th October 1835, with nine others went to the rescue of a Spanish vessel in distress 12 miles off shore. The yawls reached the ship safely, left four men on board to help man the pumps and started to return.

All went well until a squall struck the yawl and she capsized with the loss of all on board except Brock. He was plunged into the darkness in a raging sea, but was determined not to give in and, cutting away his seaman's clothes with a knife, he struck out for the shore. But he had to reckon with the tides. He kept himself afloat for seven long hours in an icy sea, being picked up by a vessel in the Corton Roads at one o' clock in the morning. He had been driven by the swell of the sea over the Cross Sand Ridge, past the buoy of St Nicholas Gat and so into the smoother water off Corton, followed all the while by flocks of screaming gulls who looked upon him as certain prey. He survived that terrible night for many years, and continued his calling as a beachman.

There is one significant thing belonging to either Suffolk or Norfolk, in the person of Henry Morris Upcher, J.P., D.L., of Eastwell Hall, Feltwell, Brandon, Suffolk, and Sheringham Hall, Sheringham, Norfolk, who was the owner of the only private lifeboat in existence.

CHAPTER XI

THE DROWNED CITY

·••✠••·
***

But you shall further understand the common fame and report of a greate number of credable persons is, and hath been for a long time paste: that there hath been in the town of Donewiche, before any decay came to it, LXX pryshe churches, howses of religion, hoppitals, and chapelles, and other such lyke, and as many wynde melles, and as many toppe scheppes, etc., but any other profe than as before is declared I have not to alledge etc. Therefore in this behalf, use yower discretion etc.

One of the highlights of a holiday at Middleton was a day at Dunwich, the nearby ruined and submerged city. One might have heard of buried cities, the result of earthquakes and eruptions, but drowned cities were certainly rare. It was a mighty long way to walk, and even more wearisome on the return journey, but usually once a year we went by pony trap. On that morning there would be all the commotion of getting ready, not forgetting the lidded basket with the provisions done up in spotless white cloths. The pony would be champing its bit, tossing its head to keep off the flies, and grandfather getting regular hotted up. Grandmother would merely see us off, hoping we would come to no grief.

Folks today, especially children, cannot enter into the joy of such a means of transport. You sat in a seat facing the horse's behind in company with the driver, or with your back to the company, watching progress from the rear. Either way there was a rug to cover your knees, your face was perched in the open air, and you were regaled with various smells of sweat, leather, oil, dust and country clothes. On the floor tucked away in case of emergency, was a huge gig umbrella covered in blue or green drill, that had a wide span when opened.

Even the trap itself was of great interest. You climbed in by means of an iron plate set on the end of a rod, and had to be careful you didn't put your hands on the iron-shod wheel, to avoid getting soiled. The woodwork was all nicely shaped with chamfered panels, and the shafts were moulded to the outline of the horse. There was a metal holder at the side by the driver which held the whip. The driver didn't use this much, it was more for show, he preferred to talk to the pony, more or less in a caressing tone. Having loaded up, we set off, and there was a noise of iron hooves trotting on a gritty road.

Now just round the corner, turning right at the signpost with its pointing finger, was a little river that burbled across the road. An old wooden footbridge at the side, probably made from ships' timbers gathered from the beach after storms, was for passengers, but vehicles forded the stream. Needless to say that on each and every occasion, the little old 'hoss' had to stop and drink, sucking up the water through its champing bit with a 'suss-suss' sort of sound. Satisfied, we passed on, climbing a bit of a hill on a winding road that was to lead us first to a three-cornered piece at the entrance to Black Slough, where the gipsies often encamped. This ancient track, as its name implied, was of black earth, lined with green hedges and green oaks.

Soon we were to pass one of Mrs Ogilvie's farms, where the stacks stood on iron staddles, that must have come out from Garrett's Leiston Works. She was a first-rate farmer, her land was clean and her stock good. Just at this point came an S-bend, and having negotiated that, we were set for Westleton Street. Arrived, we passed Ball's blacksmith's shop and could hear the music of his anvil, perhaps see the hindquarters of a horse that was being shod, and smell the burning hooves. Then came 'The Crown', a spick-and-span inn, with a Gloire de Dijon climbing over its brick front. Over the door was the name painted on the brickwork in large letters. Then at one side was a shaped board stating that George Johnson was licensed to retail beers, wines and spirits to be consumed on the premises. On the other side was a long framed board denoting the house dispensed the Colchester Brewing Company's Limited Fine Sparkling Ales and Stout. A low brick wall, surrounded the two halves of a tiny flagged path that flanked the front door. At the side was the yard, and by the backhouse a large pump with a wooden ball on the top.

Adjacent to the inn, and one would have imagined it to be one of its outbuildings, was a tiny rectangular structure some 24 feet by 15, of excoriated red brick and sand-faced tiles. It stood there forlorn and untended, with a mouldering wicket door set just above cart level in the gable-end that flanked the road. Years later I was to discover that it belonged to the fifteenth-century thatched church across the way (as probably the inn itself in the days when the Cistercian monks from Sibton held the living) and was used as a bier house. It had been used also as a mortuary, the last body resting there being of one Joe Green.

It was also a coal store, hence the wicket door set at just such a level as to be handy when unloading by skep basket the sea-borne coal that came ashore at Dunwich in the billiboy ketches. This coal was doled out to the village poor as one of the church charities, and had to be taken to the church porch for the purpose, a dole at a time, to be handed to the recipient by the parson. However, the little shed's real use was probably for the bier.

This in passing, for we were about to climb the hill out of Westleton beside the village green, to a windmill at the top, still at work. One could hear the swish of the sails as they turned, so lazily, so pleasantly, grinding local corn. Within a minute or two and we were on Westleton Common, and just at one small point between the distant trees, we could glimpse the sea and its glitter of blue water. We were entering the land of high romance, heather covered, with a lark trilling its way upwards, and the few telegraph wires of the coastguards acting as an Aeolian harp. If we had been walking we should have been looking for the Dunwich rose, or trying to catch a whiff of sweet briar. Over to the east was Racecourse Farm, owned by Colonel Barne.

Soon we should be at the turning that led to Minsmere, a pretty name, and at the five-barred gate that led to Squire Barne's mansion. This was really an old shooting box that had been added to and converted into a Victorian Tudor mansion. In the grounds were a circular covered way for exercising a horse, and a cemetery for favourite Arabs and dogs. The place was alleged to be haunted.

This corner was heavily wooded, with chestnut trees lining the way. Then there, as the road turned sharp left, stood a pillar box and a row of estate cottages. Excitement grew, because within minutes we should be passing the old rubble walls of the monastery enclosure and the two beautiful ruined gateways of the Grey Friars. Through the larger of the two we could just see the ruined church on the cliff, and we should soon know how much of it had gone since last year. But just as we passed this wonderful spot, the road dropped down and we could see the sea. There it was, sometimes as calm as a mill pond, sometimes muddling about, as the old woman said when she saw it for the first time. How comfortable to arrive so slowly, with time to look about and enjoy it all. Something impossible to this generation when there are no horses, and a car that whisks you there in a wink.

Although Dunwich was merely a cluster of little houses, entirely owned by one family, it was a thrilling place in which to be. Even as a child one felt its magic. True it was associated with death and destruction, with wild days and wilder nights, but somehow or the other it always appeared to be the same. There was an old cannon bollard at the bottom of the hill; but there was no chapel, although the Plymouth Brethren had a cell there. One went to the beach along a sandy lane, past the garden of the house on the corner, always associated with artists, where fig trees rustled their great leaves, until we came to a hut with the nameboard of a wreck over the door. Here we could get cups of tea freshly made and slices of Suffolk bread spread with Suffolk butter. By which time we were on the pebbly beach with some sandy patches on the foreshore. It is a most curious fact that once there, all we did was to sit on the beach looking seawards, content to do nothing, save perhaps to walk along the pathway on the cliff, often through standing corn, to see what had happened to the old church, examine once again the one or two gravestones and wonder how long it would be before the whole lot went over, bones and all.

When I first went to Dunwich the hut at the bottom of the lane must have been on the beach, because I can remember it standing in the sun, well away from the water. I don't know if it was kept by old Mr and Mrs Brown, or whether it had passed to the Watlings. Mr Watling was an interesting man, a fisherman, who made a wonderful collection of coins, pins and little relics of the old city which used to appear on the beach after what was known as a scouring tide. Some of these came out from the cliff face as the bones fell away from the crumbling sand. At one time well-casings appeared, standing like ancient factory chimneys, signs of some long lost hereditament, messuage or tenement.

Dunwich was indeed a place of legend and romance, with a long and fascinating story. The fragment that remained was but the western outskirts of the old city, and one was regaled with stories of hidden treasure, underground passages and buried steeples. Some, given to that psychic quality of penetration, averred they could hear the bells ringing under the water, especially so if they put their ears to the clifftop and listened. Sufficient to say, they were visitors rather than local fishermen. The latter would sometimes complain they fouled their nets on some old lump of rubble, or brought up bits and pieces that were not fish.

It is almost certain that Dunwich, situated as it is about midway along the coast, was a Roman station. If one considers the coast as coming within the defensive survey of the Roman occupiers, the circumstantial evidence would point to this. With Burgh Castle to the north and the supposed Walton Castle to the south at Felixstowe, it would be difficult not to believe that such was the case. Here at least one might suppose a signal station, part of the coastal defence under the charge of the Count of the Saxon Shore. Whatever it may have been, it must have disappeared early in the story, considering that the old city was probably a mile or two out to sea.

Dunwich has been identified with Sitomagus, but others have considered it to be too far eastwards. Confirmation of local Roman occupation, however, comes from Scotts Hall, not far from Minsmere, where a coarse earthenware pot some 8 to 10 inches high was dug up. This contained silver and brass coins of the Roman era, although too decayed to be identified. A statuette of Venus was found at Blyford bridge, near Blythburgh. Two other objects found in Dunwich itself are in the Acton Collection at Moyses Hall, Bury St Edmunds. They are described as chapes, parts of a scabbard.

The hinterland of Dunwich is the Dingle, now the happy

domain of bird lovers. This was thought to have been a meeting place of the Suffolk Thing. A writer in *East Anglian Notes and Queries*, 1889–94, suggests Dingle Great Hill as the meeting place of the Great Thing of the shire, and Dingle Little Hill for the Lesser Thing of the Hundred, perpetuated in the name of Blything. This assumption was based on the theory that Dunwich was Sitomagus.

Dunwich must have had many smuggling episodes to its credit, particularly about Minsmere and the Sluice. The last of the Dunwich smugglers was probably Elijah Larter, a lovely and local name, whose lamps are in the museum.

Many visitors of distinction made Dunwich the scene of an annual pilgrimage, or resided there. Of these was Edwin Edwards, painter and etcher (1823–79), born at Halesworth. He lived at The Ferns, opposite the 'Ship'. To his home came Edward FitzGerald, who had much regard for "the brave boy but indifferent painter and his heroic wife". Edwards taught him to play Spanish dominoes. Another visitor was Charles Keene of *Punch*, who was addicted to playing the bagpipes and sucking brandy balls. He was an inveterate smoker, using a short clay pipe with a tiny bowl. Of Fitz he said: "Just one of our sort, very bookish and fond of art and delightful company." Incidentally, Keene's mother was a Mary Sparrowe, or Sparowe, of the Ancient House, Ipswich. FitzGerald dated many of his letters from Dunwich. He stayed with one of the Dixes, and often headed the letters as from 'Dix Hall'.

Old Fitz loved Dunwich and his visits were for long a legend amongst the natives. He delighted to rise early, go and sit amidst the ruins on the cliff, wearing a tall hat. On hot days he might have been seen walking barefoot along the dusty road, nodding his head (as did all the FitzGeralds) clad in a red bandana, and carrying his boots in his hands.

Swinburne came here in 1875, when lodging at Wangford, and again in 1877. The visits inspired him to write *By the North Sea*, with a special verse for All Saints. Jerome K. Jerome was another constant visitor. It was said he was on his way here when struck down with a fatal illness. Mention too must be made of Rider Haggard, who staged one of his lesser known works here, *Red Eve*.

The Second World War came to Dunwich as it came everywhere, making of this tiny hamlet a 'closed area'. The beach was heavily barricaded and mined, the marshes blocked with concrete cubes, and Minsmere became a hush-hush radar station. A lookout for coast watchers found a vantage spot in the old churchyard on the cliff, manned by old salts such as George Darkins from his nautically-flavoured village post office. And blockhouses were built.

But perhaps the greatest occasion came with the flying bombs, let loose over the grey waters, streaking in above the ancient city. A.A. Artillery was moved here to meet the threat, and a whole battery found just sufficient room within the monastery walls— surely the strangest guests that had ever entered those gates. And be it recorded to the eternal honour of those drivers, that they manoeuvred those ponderous vehicles and lumbering guns through those old portals without doing the slightest damage to the fabric. They placed the sighting lamps on the lichened walls, chopped down the knarled and twisted trees that grew between the walls and the sea. Then, having done their job they pulled out again, to leave the place to its old memories and its ancient peace.

At Dunwich, still can be found the yellow sea poppy, the sea aster, the rare sea pea, and the sea spurge; calling to mind the words of the worthy Fuller: "To conclude our description of Suffolk, I wish that therein grain of all kinds may be had at so reasonable rates, that rich and poor may be contented therewith. But if a famine should happen here, let the poor not distrust Divine Providence, whereof their grandfathers had so admirable a testimony, 15 . . . when, in a general dearth all over England plenty of pease did grow on the sea shore near Dunwich (never set or sown by human industry) which, being gathered in full ripeness, much abated the high prices in the markets, and preserved many hundreds of hungry families from famishing."

(This had a modern rendering during the war when ships were being torpedoed, and bags of the best and whitest flour were washed ashore in a time of great scarcity from a wreck on the Goodwins.)

A little north of Dunwich was Walberswick, a name that always intrigued me, because the old locals persisted in calling it

Walserwig. It fascinated *Punch* also, who published this of it in 1880:

O Walberswick's a village of very little tillage
  In the northern part of Suffolk, and its very picturesque;
And you fly from all the gritty, dirty bye-ways of the City,
  To forget, in pleasant rambles, dreary duties of the desk.

There's a harbour old and rotten, planks and anchors long forgotten
  'Mid the tangle of the cordage: boats whose sea career is o'er;
There's a ferry with scant traffic, which McCullum and the Graphic
  Sketched long years ago, and sea-gulls sweep along the
                                    lonesome shore.

There gathers many a skecher, Dr. Eversted the Etcher,
  Stacey Marks and Haswell, Langton, Barnard and one Keene,
Who greatly love the queer place and declare it is a dear place,
  And with skilful brush and pencil they've immortalised the scene.

There's no horrible cheap tripper comes, a most persistent dipper
  In the 'briny', and Cook's tourist is unknown within these parts;
And the sunset waxing fainter o'er the church delights the painter,
  No wonder then that Walsberwick is dear to artists' hearts.

This more or less sums up the place and the atmosphere of the times.

It was possible to walk there from Dunwich by the beach or across the marshes. And as there was a beacon mound on the cliff's edge at Dunwich (surely a romantic bit for a boy), so there was another in line over against Walberswick. Besides, as it grew dusk, one could see the flash of the Southwold lighthouse just beyond.

Surely a village is remarkable when it passes into local apophthegms. For long enough the old people used to speak of a loud-mouthed person as a "Walserwig whisperer. Yow may har him oova t'Sowle". Then they enforced its peculiarity by another uncomplimentary remark, describing a person who could not keep to the point. "He's gon' ter Wanfer (Wangford) ter git tew Walserwig". Of course there were a lot of people like that. They could hold a conversation in their sing-song language, across a ten acre field, but found it difficult to reach the point, if tackled.

They were mostly poor people in Walberswick, fishing folk,

and the like, who often found it hard to make ends meet. As one remarked: "People didn't live then, they just *lingered*." When they couldn't fish they were resourceful enough to fish for anchors, because this was a rare coast for shipwrecks. Besides it delighted in folk-lore as did its neighbour, especially to do with the sea and sailors.

I must confess to a great liking for a description given by one of them of another of them, to wit Old Sarah: "She had known the day when she had only the one pair of stocken she stood up in (presumably she had other clothes as well), and not a bit of soap to wash her flesh with, nor a broom to sweep the room with, and when she ba-aked, she put the flour on the table and made a hole in it, and ba-a-ked the loaf in an old saucepan on the fire, with no handle, what some ship's crew had thrown on the beach". You couldn't get closer to Nature than that.

But there was one great attraction at Walberswick (where the air was so 'embracing' as one old lady put it), and that was the old ferry that connected it with Southwold, crossing the Blyth many times a day. It was a pontoon ferry that ran on chains from bank to bank, to ramps constructed for the purpose, and was worked by a donkey engine. Before that it was worked by hand. For many years old George Todd pulled the string that caused the whistle to shriek, and drove the load into the tide. George was one of those Walberswick characters, and there is a picture of him looking out over a half-hatch door, with a full beard, like a bird's nest, wearing what appears to be a Spanish straw hat.

All kinds of loads managed to get on to this crazy bit of transport, enclosed by a couple of rickety gates, until it looked like a piece of pilotage belonging to eastern waters. The tariff suggests its carrying capacity. "Foot passengers $1\frac{1}{2}$d; Drivers and vehicles 3d; Extra horses 2d; Persons and trucks 1d; Sheep 1d; Cattle 2d." It had a nasty habit of sinking occasionally, or the "danged owd chain" might break, but when it ended its career its loss was great.

Then, of course, there was that priceless bit of railway that ran from Southwold to Halesworth, with a station at Walberswick. That also was the butt of the Victorian punsters, but when it came to an end, its loss was irreparable. This is what T. West Carnie wrote about it in 1899.

"Nobody takes the Southwold Railway seriously, except perhaps its own officials; but as the entire personnel of the railway can be counted on the fingers of two hands, the 'officials' are in a minority. The entire distance between Halesworth and Southwold is a little over nine miles, but there are three intermediate stations: Walberswick, Blythburgh, and Wenhaston. Although there is only one train, which goes backwards and forwards, the company issues an official time-table, but, luckily, on its outside page, they 'do not guarantee that the trains will keep to the times of starting or arriving as mentioned'. At Southwold the one porter generally rings a bell when the train is going to start, and then the loiterers seat themselves; but, if you happen to get left behind, it is quite possible to run after the train and catch it up at Walberswick. This has actually been done, but, of course, in very hot weather it is more comfortable to have a seat in one of the tramcar-like carriages.

"If the distance covered by this little line is but a short one, the scenery is charming. At first, after leaving Halesworth, you pass through a richly cultivated agricultural district, where the golden corn gives fullest promise of an ample harvest. After leaving Blythburgh, however, the surroundings change, and the line traverses a wild bit of moorland, where the heather and heath are purple in the sun, and the scent of the pine trees is wafted in through the open carriage doors. At Walberswick you come in sight of the sea, and, crossing the Blyth, you pass the Southwold golf-links and enter Southwold station."

I had the luck to cross over in the old ferry, but it has been always a regret that I never had the thrill of a ride on the Southwold Railway.

CHAPTER XII

THE 1851 EXHIBITION AND THE EASTERN COUNTIES

·····ợ····

I have recently come across a copy of the *Official Catalogue of the Great Exhibition Of The Works Of All Nations, 1851*, and found it absorbing reading. This belonged to a Suffolk man who had made the pilgrimage to Hyde Park. The exhibition was a deeply religious occasion as well as being a glorious get-together of all sorts of marvellous things. It is not surprising therefore that the title page bears a verse of scripture: "The earth is the Lord's, and all that therein is: The compass of the world and they that dwell therein." This is followed by two Latin inscriptions with translations:

> Say not the discoveries we make are our own:
> The germs of every art are implanted within us.
> And God our Instructor, from hidden sources, develops the
>   Faculties of invention.

> The progress of the human race
> Resulting from the common labour of all men,
> Ought to be the final object of the exertion of each individual
>   In promoting this end,
> We are accomplishing the will of the great and blessed God.

The British exhibits were divided into thirty classes, each of which was numbered from one. Class 1 consisted of Mining and Mineral Products. Number 119 was by F. Fisher of Woolpit, who showed specimens of Woolpit brick earth, which was of a white gault nature. He also showed some building bricks, pamment bricks and drainage pipes. Pamment was an old Suffolk word for a thin square whitish brick, for pavements. Many a Suffolk floor and pantry were paved with them; but the Woolpit bricks, which were largely used, were frowned upon by the aesthetes.

We now pass to Class 2, for Chemical and Pharmaceutical Products, where we find number 38, T. Spurgin of Saffron Walden, showing the root, stem, flower and stigmata of the saffron plant. This, of course, was used medicinally, and at that time as a cure for gout, and also in cooking for saffron cakes.

Number 90, J. H. Kent of Stanton near Bury St. Edmunds, showed various dried pharmaceutical indigenous plants in glass vessels, with extracts.

This brings us to Class 3. Substances used as food. Number 2 was by H. Doubleday of Coggeshall, Essex, who exhibited some fine speciments of honeycomb. This is not surprising when one remembers the seed beds for which Coggeshall was noted, aflame with colour—something for the bees to work upon.

Then number 70 must have delighted the farmers, because A. Sheppard of Ipswich, showed Eggshell white wheat and Chevallier malting barley, grown in Suffolk and malted in Ipswich.

He was followed by number 73, R. Raynbird of Hengrave, near Bury St. Edmunds, who produced Kessingland wheat grown on the light land of Hengrave which is close to Suffolk Breckland. He also favoured Chevallier barley, and tick beans with white eyes, all grown at Hengrave.

Number 88, S. Cousens of Great Bentley, near Colchester, came up with a new variety of White Wheat, an imperial bushel of which weighed 64 pounds nett.

Number 107A comes from H. Wright of Antingham, near North Walsham. He was a maltster who showed his product manufactured from barley grown by the Revered C. Creemer of Beeston, near Cromer, Norfolk. Barley was a considerable crop, and there were a number of maltings tucked away in outlying places in Suffolk and Norfolk, almost as many as the oast houses in Kent.

Number 152, E. Marriage of Colchester brought samples of flour, a firm that is with us today. The same by 160, F. C. Fitch, of Steeple Bumpstead, Essex, who exhibited wheaten flour, manufactured from Essex wheat.

Class 4 was for Vegetable and Animal Substances used in Manufactures in which number 119 was a display by T. C. and G. Swinburne and Co. of Coggeshall and No. 1 Gt. Tower

Street, London, of refined isinglass, gelatines and glues. Do you remember when eggs were in abundance and cheap they were pickled in isinglass; usually in a great earthenware pot, as used for pickling belly pork?

Number 121 was a show by Abbott and Wright of Needham Market. They specialized in Crown glue as made from the hides and feet of cattle. This could not have produced a very pleasant smell, but must have been a by-product of the tanning then carried on in this neighbourhood.

Class 5 was for Machines, a definite product of the Industrial Revolution. The machinery of Suffolk was almost exclusively agricultural, and was famous throughout the world. The first name was number 30, Ransomes and May of Ipswich, with a 5 horse-power steam engine. This would have been a fixed engine.

Number 402, W. Shalders junior of Bank Place, Norwich, showed Patent fountain pumps, engines and hydraulic work.

Number 640 is another show by Ransomes and May, this time for the spreading network of railways. This included Barlow and Heald's railway turn-tables, Wild's railway turn-tables and switch. Barlow's iron sleepers, Registered water crane. Patent compressed treenails, Legatt's Queen press, with self-inking apparatus. And a chilled cast-iron pedestal, or axle bearing. Incidentally, treenail was a very old word for a wooden wedge. It was a term used for the wooden pins used in the construction of the timber-framed houses, instead of iron nails.

Number 681, J. A. Tabor of Colchester, demonstrated an improved application of the whistle to locomotive engines, and the proper application thereof to steamboats. Those old engines, steaming through the quiet countryside, could be heard miles away, when they used their whistles. It was often a sign of rain. That is something that now belongs entirely to the past.

We now come to number 892, which shows the extent of this class which reached 998 exhibits in all. This was made by K. Kent of Saffron Walden, Essex, who showed a Carriage with a low body, forming an invalid's pony chaise.

Class 6 was for Manufacturing Machines and Tools, which provided only two numbers from the Eastern Counties, both from Ipswich. Number 146, Ransomes and May, a Model of a patent

Rectory Lane, Earl Stonham

The back of the 'White Hart', Blythburgh in 1892

excavator for railways or canals. Models of improved apparatus and machinery, for preparing timber with creosote, etc.

Number 414, G. Hurwood, Ipswich, showed Various patent metal mills for grinding corn, pulse, spices etc. A Plate showing the grinding surface of a mill and a Stone case, with apparatus for supplying air to the grinding surface of mill stones.

This carries us naturally to Class 7, for Civil Engineering, Architecture and Building Contrivancies, with number 31, again filled by G. Hurwood of Ipswich. He exhibited a window made to open and close in one and several parts by the application of the patent apparatus. It was used for the ventilation of the Exhibition building. Various models showing the mode of applying the invention to different windows. He also showed Patent ship-lights and scuttles, and a Model and drawing of a breakwater.

Number 49, P. Bruff of Ipswich, Designer, showed a model for a proposed national harbour of refuge on the east coast of England. He was the man who engineered the railway line from Ipswich to Colchester, for the old Eastern Union Railway.

Class 8, was for Naval Architecture, Military Engineering, Guns, Weapons etc, with number 16, producing a Life-Boat by C. Hall of Lowestoft. He is followed by number 22, G. W. Manby of Great Yarmouth, with his Life-Boat and mortar apparatus. He invented the apparatus for saving lives from ship-wrecks. Captain Manby's life-saving apparatus was supplied to every station on our coasts.

Number 25, was occupied by D. Offord of Great Yarmouth. He showed Grapnell shot, to assist the hauling of life boats etc, off the beach through heavy surfs.

Number 26, follows again by D. Offord and S. Bradbeer, with Rock life-preserving apparatus.

Number 37, G. R. Tovell of Mistley, Manningtree, Essex, showed a model of a ship's hull of parabolical form.

Number 129, Commander F. A. Ellis, R.N., of Great Yarmouth, had a Model of a yacht with a sliding keel, to enable her to go up shallow rivers and over bar harbours. Also a method of lowering the mast, and a projecting bow, etc. I think these were for use by explorers.

Class 9 was for Agricultural and Horticultural Machines and

Implements. Number 17, A. F. Campbell of Plumpstead, Norfolk, showed a Patent four-wheel parallel motor harrow.

Number 32, J. Bendall of Woodbridge, had a universal self-adjusting cultivator, for skimming, cleaning, pulverizing, or sub-soiling land. And a corn crushing machine for beans, peas, barley, etc.

Number 37, C. Burrell of Thetford showed a very interesting and rather novel collection, with a 6-horse-power portable steam-engine, adapted for drawing agricultural machinery. Also a registered machine for making hurdles or gates. And a registered gorse-cutting and brusing machine.

Number 80, R. F. Swan of Boxford, Suffolk, showed a Model of a tipping waggon.

Number 82, J. Woods of Stowmarket, exhibited a New universal farmer's crushing and grinding mill.

Number 92, W. J. Pettit of Sudbury, displayed a Temple and collateral beehives. This sounds rather grand.

Now comes number 124, Ransomes and May of Ipswich, with Patent iron ploughs, double breast or moulding ploughs; West Indian, double furrow, universal, broad share and subsoil ploughs; trussed whippletrees; Biddell's scarifier; Indian cultivator; corn and seed dropping machine, portable steam engines; fixed steam engine; thrashing machines; cane-top cutter; Scotch cart, etc. Altogether this must have been a very large exhibit.

It was followed by number 142, Garrett and Sons, Leiston Works, Suffolk, with drills, horse-hoes, thrashing machines, portable steam-engines hummelling and corn dressing machines, chaff cutters, crushers, ploughs, corn-reaping harrows and other agricultural machinery. Hummellers were used for taking off the awms of barley. Garretts' developed a large export business with Russia and South America.

Number 182, E. R. Turner of Ipswich, showed a 4-horse-power portable engine for agricultural purposes. An apparatus for regulating the supply of water to a high-pressure steam boiler. Also a Mill for crushing corn and seeds, and grinding beans, peas, maize, etc.

Number 269, C. E. Jones, B.A., came up with The Cottager's double beehive, with regulating doorway to the floorboard. 2, Rim for enlarging the hive. This I give for its interest and not because it comes from the Eastern Counties. Cottagers *per se*, existed in those days.

Number 216, R. Coleman of Chelmsford, had a Patent drag harrow and scarifier. Also a Patent subsoil harrow and Patent expanding lever harrow.

Number 217 E. H. Bentall, of Heybridge, near Maldon, Essex showed a Patent broad-share and subsoil plough. A Patent mangel and ridge hoe, Patent double tom, with wrought-iron beam. A Patent N.G.H. plough, the original gold hanger plough and Patent dynamometer, etc. He was of the family that created Bentall's of Kingston.

Number 257, J. Warren of Heybridge, near Maldon, Essex, Inventor and designer, produced a Vegetation hoe, Alarum guns, etc., Skim plough for hoeing and cleaning land.

Number 259, C. Burcham of Heacham, near Lynn, had a model of a steam and human-power cultivator, or universal tillage machine and irrigator.

And one exhibitor showed a Norfolk dock or thistle extractor.

Class 10, was for Philosophical and Musical Instruments. Number 117, J. Price of Bury St. Edmunds, must have attracted a good deal of attention with his Skeleton Clock which goes three years. Pyramidical skeleton timepiece, which goes three months. He also showed Barometers.

Number 680 brings us again to D. Offord, of Great Yarmouth, with an improved truss for hernia. And improved instruments for the treatment of uterine diseases.

I give the remainder as listed:

Classes 12 and 15. *Woollen and Worsted, Mixed Fabrics, Including Shawls.*

No. 225. Allen, G. Norwich. Glove clothes.

No. 226. Allen & Banks, Norwich. East Anglian cloths manufactured from Norfolk wool. Presumably from the old Norfolk horned sheep.

No. 284. Clabburn & Son, Norwich. Registered figured Cashmere shawls. Spun-silk fancy check, and Albanian silk shawls. Registered Jacquard figured poplin, and chiné poplins; and mixed fabrics. etc.

No. 285. Blakely, E. T. River House Factory, Dukes' Place, Norwich. Norwich cashmere green scarf shawl, gold introduced.

Shawls of Cashmere, design by John Funnell. Anglo Indian scarfs, shawls, dresses, brocades etc.

No. 286. Towler, Campin & Co., Elm Hill, Norwich and 46 Friday St. London. Villover scarves; silk ground. Printed silks, and silk net shawls. Ladies' paletots, worked to fit the shape.

No. 309. Fowler, Campin & Co., Norwich challi. Satin striped de laines, Paramatta cloth and Barège for dresses.

No. 310. Willet, E. Nephew & Co. Norwich. Mixed fabrics for dresses consisting of bombazines and paramattas, poplins, brocades, chinés etc. A mixed fabric, composed of materials from nine different countries.

No. 311. Bolingbroke C & F. Norwich. Plain and watered poplins.

No. 312. Middleton & Ainsworth, Norwich and London. Poplin corded and brocaded, and black paramattas.

No. 313. Hinde, E. & F. Norwich, Barèges and brocaded poplins.

No. 500. H.R.H. Prince Albert—Two brocaded dresses, two shawls and a specimen of coarse cloth, the weft of the dresses and the shawls and cloth entirely of cashmere wool, from goats kept in Windsor Park. [Given for its interest.]

Class 16. *Leather, Saddlery, Boots and Shoes.*

No. 178. Winter, C. Norwich. Ladies' elegant boots and shoes.

No. 264. Tyzack, W. V., Norwich. Specimens of false hair. (Why false when there was plenty of human about?)

No. 275. Cox, T. Buff Court Lane, Norwich. Pony harness and fancy baskets, woven from flax grown in Norfolk.

Class 17. *Paper, Printing and Bookbinding.*

No. 199. Gardener, W. H., Troy House, Manningtree, Essex. Specimen of penmanship. Could he have been a writing master?

Class 19. *Tapestry, Floor Cloths, Lace and Embroidery.*

No. 241. Lee, A. J. A specimen of lace made by a poor woman in Stone, Aylesbury. [Given for its interest.]

No. 384. Kiddle, J. Norwich. Woven cushion, completed in the loom without the aid of needlework.

Class 21. *Cutlery, Edge and Hand Tools.*

No. 28. Offord D. Great Yarmouth. Improved masticating knife and fork for dyspeptic persons, etc.

Class 22. *General Hardware, Including Locks and Grates.*

No. 34. Barnard & Bishop, Norwich. Galvanised iron wire netting. Wrought-iron hinge.

No. 440. Harvey, G. Great Yarmouth. Ship's stove.

No. 556. Gidney, J. W., East Dereham, Norfolk. Models of improved wire-fence, and portable iron sheepfold. Ornamental castings, for gates, palisading, etc. Door with lever-spring drop, to exclude the draught; invented and registered by M. Gardener of Ashill, Norfolk. Hemispherical stove, designed, registered and manufactured by Barwell & Co, of Northampton. Model of greenhouse.

No. 575. Bradnack, I. R. Great Yarmouth. Summer skates, adapted for a macadamised road etc. Improved knocker, letter plate etc, for a door.

No. 675. Downs, W., Long Melford, near Sudbury, Suffolk. Improved twelve-bolt lock, to be fastened on the centre of a door, three bolts shooting each way.

Class 24 was for Glass, and number 45, W. Beningfield, Colchester, Essex, showed a Glass picture-frame of an original design; the gilding or other ornamental work being completely protected.

Class 26. *Furniture, Upholstery, Paper Hangings, Papier Mache and Japanned Goods.*

No. 36. Fisher, J. W., Calvert Street, Norwich. Loo-table, in veneers of English growth, viz. walnut tree curls, and intersected with laburnum tree.

No. 38. Freeman, W. & C., London Street, Norwich. An ornamental cabinet, secretary and bookcase, carved in walnut wood and ebony.

No. 39. Puxley, W., Norwich. Ornamental flower table, slate top, carved maple and knotted oak-wood border, with dial affixed showing the time on the top of the table.

No. 40. Fonnereau, Kate G. Ipswich, Octagon box, in imitation of inlaid wood applicable to pianofortes.

No. 41. Hanbury, Louisa Emily, Ipswich. Slab in imitation of marble, supported by carving in wood.

No. 42. Ringham, H. Carr St. Ipswich. Rood screen, carved in oak for a church in Surrey, designed by J. Clarke, 13, Stratford Place, London. Group of wheat and poppies, carved in lime wood.

No. 45. Abbot, J. Horse and Groom, Crouch Street, Colchester. Inlaid pentagon table. Inlaid table with carved pedestal, the sole work of the exhibitor, a blacksmith.

No. 66. Stopher, T. Saxmundham. Reading, writing and dressing desks.

No. 83. Aggio, G. H., Colchester. White and gold ottoman, embossed wool and silk, in glass case.

Class 27. *Manufactures in Mineral Substances, for Building or Decorations.*

No. 5. Frewer, J. Woodbridge Road, Ipswich. A Caen stone carved chimney-piece.

No. 101. Laurie, W., Downham Market, Suffolk, Sculptor. Models of Christian memorials. etc. [This should read Norfolk, not Suffolk.]

No. 111. Luft, J. Tuddenham, Ipswich. Ornamental chimney shafts, and red bricks; red and white ornamental bricks, ridge-tiles, paving tiles, malt kiln tiles etc.

No. 126. Key, E. S. Bale, Dereham, Norfolk. White and red brick window frames; glazed valley tiles, manufactured by W. Colman, Swanton Novers.

No. 128. Ambrose, J., Copford, near Colchester. Gothic chimneys of red and white bricks and manufactured clay.

Class 28. *Manufactures from Animal and Vegetable Substances not being Woven or Felted.*

No. 35. Lee, F., Shippham, Norfolk. Carved oak lectern of flamboyant or late decorated styles.

No. 141. Garrett, 1 Victorian Terrace, Woodbridge Road, Ipswich. Ornamental turned snuff boxes in ivory, and fancy foreign woods.

Class 29. *Miscellaneous Manufactures and Small Wares.*

No. 26. Faiers, J. 154 High Street, Colchester. Vegetable oil for perfumery.

No. 102. Gower, T. Gun Lane, St. Stephen's, Norwich. Lemonade prepared from vegetable substances.

No. 161. Dennis, Rev. J. B. P., Bury St. Edmunds. Peacock with train spread (copy from nature). Small gull.

No. 168. Harmer H. R., Great Yarmouth. Net for keeping fish alive.

Class 30. *Sculpture, Models, and Plastic Art. Mosaics, Enamels etc.*

No. 26. Sillett, J. Kelsale, Saxmundham. Model of ground floor cottage, designed and built by the exhibitor for himself at the cost of £65.

No. 38. Cowell, S. H., Ipswich. Specimens of anastatic printing, as applied to original drawings in chalk or ink, ancient deeds, wood engravings, archaeological illustrations etc.

No. 220. Mechi, J. J., Tiptree Hall farmery, near Kelvedon, Essex. Working model of Tiptree Hall farmery: the model by H. S. Merrett, 83 Fetter Lane, London; the machinery of the model by

G. F. Campbell, 17 Addington St. York Road, Lambeth. The models of animals by Vincenzo Ruffoni and Forzano, 4 Greville Street, Hatton Garden.

No. 298. Harmer H. R., Great Yarmouth. Four "sun" pictures.

No. 331. Chancellor, F., Chelmsford. Model of a covered homestall for a farm of from 300 to 500 acres, exhibiting an improved arrangement.

It is a long time now since this truly Great Exhibition closed its doors and the exhibits were dispersed. Realizing they were all new and the latest things out, one may well ask what has become of them? I suppose the machinery and the startling innovations produced by Ransomes and May have gone for scrap, after rusting away in old farmyards. Even Tabor's locomotive whistle must have blown its last blast. Is Chevallier barley still harvested? It was considered a fine seed and much used.

Is the skeleton clock that went for three years still going or did it stop, never to go again? Or has it become a museum piece? What about the cashmere shawls from Norwich, great grandmother's pride and joy? Have they all become fretted with moth, or do some survive as family treasures? (It was Queen Victoria who popularized the use of the plaid shawl as a garment for women.) What about the paletots (a loose overcoat); the bombazines (a twilled and corded fabric of silk and worsted, or cotton and worsted)? Have they all gone into the rag bag? You might find some on display at museums like the Victoria and Albert. And what can have happened to Tyzack's specimen of false hair?

And why did Miss Kate Fonnereau exhibit an octagon box, size not stated, or Miss Hanbury show a slab of imitation marble, supported by carving? These were hardly drawing-room attainments. What then was the purport of a specimen in penmanship? It was taught us at school long after the exhibition closed. But I like the reference to "Four 'sun' pictures" from Yarmouth, because photography was in its infancy, especially outdoor scenes. Then there was the masticating knife and fork. I wonder if they cured anyone's drooping spirits after eating? They might have done so by suggestion if not by labial action. And wouldn't you like to know what happened to the two tables, the sole work of the blacksmith at Colchester? Or the intriguing, evidently working, model of the Tiptree Hall farmery. There were such models at the old palace when I went there with my father, penny in the slot.

One thing seems quite certain, that J. Sillett's ground-floor cottage designed and built by himself at Kelsale near Saxmundham, must be still there. It would appear fitting if a plaque could be affixed announcing the fact that a model of this was shown at the Great Exhibition of 1851, and greatly admired. But remember, to its eternal credit that it was Ipswich that provided the ventilating to that vast and wonderful building, vide Class 7, No. 31. And remember much of the raw material used by the Norwich weavers would have come out from Suffolk looms

> Glacier-diamond, Alp of glass,
> Sinbad's cave, Aladdin's Hall,—
> Must it then be crush'd, alas!
> Must the Crystal Palace fall?

CHAPTER XIII

A NATIONAL SCHOOL LOG BOOK FOR
1876–95

···☙···

It were better to perish than to continue schoolmastering.

Carlyle.

A neatly bound volume of a Suffolk school record has just come
my way. It makes excellent reading of the early years of compulsory education, the difficulties of enforcing the law, the
counter attractions in the way of earning something on the side—
at the local golf course, perhaps, or donkey driving on the beach.
Truancy was all too common, and there was always a difficulty in
collecting the penny or 2d. a week in fees. Emphasis is interesting,
because needlwork loomed large for the girls, overlooked and
encouraged by the ladies of the parish. One of the latter, who was
extremely active, being Mrs Allenby, mother of the Field
Marshal. The vicar's wife took the weekly Scripture lesson, while
the vicar and his curates visited the school.

Although now suburbanised, Felixstowe was then a village
surrounded by corn fields. The summer holidays were 'harvest'
holidays; only in later years did they come to be termed
vacations. Gleaning in the fields kept the children beyond the
allotted span. Flower shows called for a half holiday; but many
took French leave as occasion demanded. Local events are
recorded, such as the opening of the Felixstowe railway, while
the weather is not left out as it affects school attendances. The
surprising thing is the list of local names that are still with us, so
characteristic of endemic village life. The years were so often
disturbed by epidemics, sanitation was primitive, and the school-
rooms draughty. Class distinction was very much observed.

During the period under review there were three school-
masters, one at least resigning because he could get so little

support from the board of governors. Also two vicars died during the period. However, taking it all in all, in spite of the faults of the school, the boys and girls with all their misdemeanours became excellent citizens, of whom their descendants have every reason to be proud. The extracts are taken in chronological order, but names are omitted.

October 2, 1876. The Walton and Felixstowe National School having been transferred to the Walton United District School Board; the usual weekly entries will be made in this book instead of the old log book.

Robt. Bramwell (Schoolmaster).

October 6. The week began with a good attendance but after Wednesday it fell off considerably. Mrs. Maunder (the Vicar's wife) gave the usual Scripture lesson on Monday morning. The needle-woman was away on Friday afternoon.

October 27. During the past week the timetable has not been strictly adhered to as the school has been working with a regard to the Examinations which took place to-day, several things in which they were backward wanting particular attention. The examination began at 10.30 and was over by 1.45. The extra subjects were Geography, Grammar and Needlework.

November 3. The children have been very troublesome this week consequent no doubt on their having been moved up in classes. The Rev. C. Maunder visited on Tuesday.

November 10. The wintry weather of yesterday and to-day has pulled down the average for the week. On Monday a $\frac{1}{2}$ holiday was given, the room being required for the Clothing Club.

November 17. Two boys who truanted till Wednesday afternoon and then came late, were told to remain away the rest of the week.

December 8. I have admitted 21 children from Felixstowe and have taken off 12 Walton children under the age of five. I find the Felixstowe children very backward.

December 15. Four more children from Felixstowe have been admitted this week. The children from Felixstowe attend far more regularly than those from Walton. Several afternoons this week it has been so dark that we were compelled to close the school a little before the usual time.

December 22. Christmas holidays 2 weeks.

1877.

January 12. A new scale of school fees came in force this week they are as follows. Children of Shopkeepers & Mastermen 4d. each child. Skilled artisans 2d. each child. Common Labourers 2d each for the first two children, and all the rest 1d. each. What an extraordinary reflection on the times, class distinction at its very worst! It was all too unctuously remarked that the poor old labourers were 'common'. How every one would scream to-day.

February 2. At the Board meeting on Wednesday it was determined to charge Mr. W. of Walton Ferry 2d each for his children during 6 months of the year and 4d. each during the other 6 months.

February 19. The Needlework is somewhat curtailed, it having been taught up to the present every afternoon in the week and all the afternoon.

March 2. G. B. has been expelled the school for acting indecently towards a little girl.

March 17. Hearing from Mrs. Maunder that a child in Cage Lane is suffering from Scarlatina while its brothers and sisters are attending the school, I thought it expedient to send them home till the child is well.

March 23. On Monday morning I sent home a boy from Queen Street having ascertained that there was a case of fever in the house.

April 6. The Rs refuse to pay the School Fees for the week they were sent home on account of illness in the family.

April 20. Great attention has been paid this week to the cleanliness of the children especially their boots.

May 4. On Tuesday owing to the opening of the Ipswich and Felixstowe Railway very few children came to school in the afternoon. I therefore closed the school giving them the half holiday.

May 18. Whitsuntide Holidays. 1 week.

June 1. Examination. Many of the Parents sent flowers to decorate the school, some of them very beautiful among the best were those sent by Messrs Spurling, Thurston, Versey and Durrant, all of Felixstowe.

June 29. Weather very hot children languid.

July 13. On Tuesday last I was accused of having beaten black and blue a boy. The father came round and abused me. As I had not in any way touched the child I sent for the policeman and had the affair openly investigated so that so false an accusation might as far as possible be deprived of its injurious effects in the village. [So there was trouble on that score even then, but no prosecutions or public outcries.]

July 27. The weather is now very hot and has its effect on the school. [Weather was more intense in those days, very hot summers, cold winters.]

August 3. The Board granted a half holiday on Wednesday in

consequence of the choir treat being held on that day.

August 10. Harvest Holiday, five weeks.

September 21. On Wednesday in consequence of the Annual Flower Show the afternoon's holiday was given.

October 12. There is a great deal of sickness in the two villages. I am obliged to keep in several of the boys to do their home lessons before they leave school in the afternoon as otherwise I cannot get them done at all.

October 19. The sickness (Scarlet fever) has greatly increased in the village.

December 14. The school continues to grow less, the illness called mumps is spreading.

1878.

February 1. Explusion for bad attendance, one boy, two girls. [Probably much welcomed by the culprits.]

February 22. It seems to be the custom among the Felixstowe children to stay away every Friday afternoon. [I wonder why? It couldn't have been shopping for mother.]

March 1. On Tuesday owing to the funeral of Mr. Allenby, all the Felixstowe children but 3 were away all day, and to-day it is wet, they are all away again. [How they loved a funeral in those days. This was Lord Allenby's father.]

March 22. I have had occasion to send a boy home several times lately to clean himself. [No bathrooms in those days, only a bowl on a bench out of doors.]

April 4. I had occasion this morning to find fault with the sweeping of the School; for some time past it has been done very badly, and when I sent for the woman to come and see to it she refused to do so. [Alas, Mrs Mops, the same as ever.]

April 12. Four boys have been admitted this week from Felixstowe New Town. They are all very backward, never having attended any school regularly.

June 28. I have this day expelled a boy for grossly immoral conduct in the playground.

July 19. On Wednesday a half holiday was given on the occasion of the opening of the New Organ at Walton Church.

July 26. Yesterday the school was closed in the afternoon owing to their being a review at Felixstowe.

August 2. The heat during the week has been very great.

September 13. The school reopened after the Harvest holidays with a very poor attendance. It is partly caused by the gleaning which was not quite finished.

September 20. Flower Show on Wed. ½ holiday.

October 25. The attendance this week has been very poor, today we close the old school-room. Next week will be a holiday to allow of moving up to the New schools.

November 8. Last Monday the new schools were opened. The school rooms appear to be well ventilated are very comfortable, but there is a considerable echo which increases the noise in the school.

November 15. The attendance has been surprisingly regular considering the weather, which has been wet beyond anything I have experienced since I have been in Walton.

November 22. Col. Tomline visited the school. [He was the great landowner who built the railway.]

November 29. Teachers and myself are to take in turns to watch the children during the dinner hour to prevent them running wild and damaging the school furniture.

December 13. The weather during the week has been very severe, with snow on the ground.

December 19. Christmas holidays, 2 weeks.

1879

January 24. To-day a number of boys stayed away to slide on Burrow's Pond.

January 31. On Wednesday three boys were brought before the Board for using obscene language to the girls.

March 7. A boy was detected picking the pockets of the coats hanging in the lobby on Thursday morning; the same lad on Sunday last broke open the Missionary box at the Chapel and stole the contents.

April 4. On Monday and Tuesday it was not possible to have the white needlework out on account of the high winds blowing the soot down the chimneys.

April 25. Mrs Allenby visited for the first time this week on the Ladies' Committee.

May 23. The school was closed on account of a severe attack of Measles in both Walton and Felixstowe, 20 families affected, and it was rapidly spreading.

August 1. On Wednesday afternoon the school was closed owing to most teachers going to the Choir Treat at Westerfield.

1880.

February 27. I feel more and more the necessity for curtains or some other arrangement to deaden the echo.

April 9. A boy will not attend school, and a girl who is under 12 and has not passed the 3rd. Standard has gone to service on the Terrace.

May 14. A boy played truant, and when brought back refused to work and again played truant in the afternoon.

June 25. On Thursday a half holiday was given when the bell was rung at 1.30 only 21 children put in an appearance, owing to a thunderstorm.

August 6. On Wednesday a half holiday was given owing to the Wesleyans and Baptists keeping the Sunday School Centenary.

November 19. A boy was again readmitted to the school, he seems to have made no progress since he left and I doubt if he ever will.

November 26. Mr. F. was summond for the non-attendance of a boy. He attended school yesterday in a most filthy condition, he was so disgusting that I was obliged to put him by himself, to-day he has not been at all.

December 3. Two boys have been summoned to attend before the Magistrates for having broken into a shop on the Beach.

December 17. The Board have stated that those children who have their dinner at school must be willing to assist in cleaning up the crumbs made.

1881.

January 21. Owing to the weather the school was closed on Wednesday. It was quite impossible for the children to make their way through the snow.

June 17. A thick rope has been suspended from end to end of the large room to try and stop the echo.

October 1. The attendances this week show an improvement, but there are still 40 absent on the average. Many have not returned at all and not a few are at work.

October 14. H.M.I. visited the school and gave notice of the special examination of 5 girls in needlework. Alice Markham, Julia Canham, Louisa Plant, Annie Stringer, Eva Canham.

1882.

February 24. Three weeks since I recorded the best attendance since the commencement of the School year, it has since declined and I have this week to record one of the worst averages of the year.

March 10. Two members of the Board have been investigating a case of punching or kicking supposed to have been done by a boy. The boy is now lying hopelessly ill from the effects of the blow administered on the 15th. December last.

April 21. A number of boys have taken to Golfing, they go down to the links to endeavour to get a job and if they do not succeed they cannot return in time for afternoon school.

May 12. The Inspection of the School took place by A. J. Swinburne. The needlework was taken in the afternoon, also the singing. [He was a relation of the poet's, and wrote an excellent book on the "Memories of a School Inspector".]

June 9. A family were troublesome this morning came ¾ hour late and refused to be punished and were impudent, the younger one asked to leave the room this aft. and then ran off.

June 16. Tuesday a half holiday was given in consequence of the Wesleyans holding their Sunday School treat.

June 30. On Wednesday morning owing to the Athletic Sports at Landguard Fort it was necessary to close the School in the afternoon.

July 21. There is only one part of the year when the attendance in this school is at all satisfactory, viz. the early summer when the weather is fine and before the visitors arrive.

July 28. On Thursday the school was closed owing to the funeral of the Rev. C. Maunder, Vicar of Walton and Felixstowe.

Wires to destroy the echo are not yet up though I believe they are ordered.

October 18. To-day Col. Tomline distributed the prizes.

December 8. The attendance is very bad owing to the closing of the Dock works, several of the families, who came into the place are leaving again.

The Headmaster, Robert Bramwell left. Succeeded by Mr. Edward Hargreaves.

1883.

January 8. A boy cannot tell his letters. Another boy appears "non compos mentis", and 10 others totally failed in Arithmetic, many in writing from a printed tablet.

Three dinners being stolen, baskets etc are place in sight.

Two boys found standing on closet seats punished by being made to clean them after school.

Master warned some boys about stealing turnips from a field adjoining school.

February 14. Irregularity is very great in every class, boys golfing or working, seem to defy the law and do as they like. Four boys 25 mins late, marble playing, punished. One boy seems to be the leader.

March 12. Mr and Mrs Hargreaves (master) give 3 months notice. Col. Tomline asks them to stay. The names of some of those at school were: Gildersleeves, Cutting, Branch, Durrant, Topple,

Soames, Capon, Beal, Gorham, Jennings, Crane, Francis, Bugg, Ramsay, Aldis, Bloomfield, Emeny, Catt, Secombe, Backhouse, Finboro, Knight, Turtle, Studd and Andrews.

April 12. The Master to encourage the punctuality and shew that he valued the children's efforts to be present at 9 a.m. at close of this afternoon's sessions gave each scholar an orange = 194, and scrambled away 2 pecks of barcelona nuts.

April 30. A number of the biggest girls have begun a plan of being unpunctual in the afternoons; all save one girl bringing their dinner. The reasons assigned are "gathering flowers & do not know the time", or going to "Walton to buy sweets", or "to meet some other school mate".

May 9. A girl being very inattentive at reading this A.M. standing and smiling round the class told to sit down and write 5th. Comt. on her slate. She called aloud she did not know it.

May 24. Have heard that a new "So called Ladies' School" has opened nr. Beach.

June 11. New work began in every class; its progress retarded by the continuous plan of being at home (helping mother, minding Baby, or doing nothing) 2 or 3 days per week; the fine weather, visitors at the "Annual Yacht Match", the "practising of Militia for Sports" have all told on the attendance.

July 8. Because of waste of water & continual pumping away at noon, Master has placed 6 milking tins for use & a yard monitor leaving a clean new pail full of water & seeing the Infants have a "full pail" to wash every day. Two new scholars from a Dame's School can't write a letter properly, nor make even figures, & only just tell their letters tho' 7 yrs.

July 10. A boy punished for stone throwing at noon at some girls.

October 5. There was a "Golfing Match" on Wednesday, & a large number of boys are absent.

1884.

January 21. Several Ladies on a visit to Duchess of Grafton asked leave to see the working of the School. Asked to hear them singing and were much pleased therewith. [They were from the famous Euston Hall.]

February 4. A large pane of glass over door of Girls' passage was broken at Noon and Master found two boys in backyard, one having thrown a stone thro.

April 16. Dr. Havell's concert. Because of room being required early Scripture lesson not taken. These concerts cause heavy extra work, before and after.

William Pipe in the
south porch of
Theberton Church

Johnny Hayward,
butcher of Needham
Market, in his everyday
dress

The lifeboat that went to church

Dunwich church ruins

May 9. Having cautioned certain scholars about putting pebbles into drinking pail under pump & washing hands therein. Set the pump monitor to take names and punished a number for repeating such offences. Two boys at close of this p.m. school made a very, very improper use of Drinking Pail, another pail substituted for it.

May 16. Two boys truants, yet mother sent word thro' Donkey-driving.

May 27. Enquiry from a Genm. to see if we could aid him in tracing some damage done by a "Catapault", the use of which I stopped last year.

June 10. Three boys so very dirty (appeared to have come as totally unwashed for several days) were sent to wash in School passage; have before spoken to them of not being clean their mother being ill & from home.

June 19. Finding a boy's hands, wrists and parts of both arms & face very dirty called up his brother. At night the father came—abused the Master.

June 25. A mother sends word that son is truanting & has had school fees twice & spent it. He is an "incorrigible" & fit for an Industrial School.

June 26. Mr and Mrs Hargreaves resigned, chiefly because they could get no support from the Board.

October 10. Mr. W. H. Stephens commenced duties as Head Master.

October 16. For some time past I have had complaints from boys who have had their dinners stolen from their bags whilst hanging in the porch. Last week no less than seven dinners were stolen. I watched once or twice but did not succeed in discovering the thief. However on Monday morning my watch proved successful and the culprit turned out to be a boy from Standard III. The corporal punishment administered consisted of three strokes on each hand.

1886.

April 9. Several of the boys took part in a paper chase during Friday's dinner time. The two hounds going beyond their limit laid down for them caused several boys to be very late in the afternoon.

September 10. Many children away gleaning.

October 8. Blackberrying is now a source of irregularity.

1888.

January 30. School reopened this morning after remaining closed for 6 wks.

May 11. Two boys away all the week scaring crows.

1890.
November 28. Heavy fall of snow only a dozen children turned up.

1891.
September 18. A girl who has attended a private school, works addition by putting down strokes represented by each figure and then counting them.

1892.
September 16. Miss Page from Walton Post Office attended the school for the purpose of issuing Bank Books and adding to accounts in exchange for Postage Stamp Slips.

1893.
January 20. As the late vicar of Walton and Felixstowe the Rev. H. Marriott was interred on Monday afternoon the schools were closed.
September 11. The girls have been transferred to a separate department under a Head Mistress.

1895.
April 30. The last of the school year.

THE TWILIGHT ENDING

·•◦✿◦•·

I was particularly impressed recently when watching a television programme introducing an exhibition of early photographs to be told that the Victorian era was the first to provide a portrait of eminent people for the ordinary person to see and become acquainted with. For example, it was the first reign when her ordinary subjects could see their Queen and become familiar with her face and form. This was a startling fact that had never entered my thoughts.

Then reading an account of the London Library, I came across a phrase describing the portrait of a former chief librarian as being a typical late Victorian face, made formidable by whiskers. This, of course, I could understand, since I possess a Victorian album of celebrities, the sort of portfolio that graced, or littered, a Victorian drawing-room, although I should never have thought of describing a face as Victorian.

It was generally feared and spoken of almost apprehensively at the time, that the death of the old Queen was indeed the end of an era. Although this was undoubtedly the case, it was not quite so sudden as that, because the period succeeding might have been described as twilight years, leading up to the first Great War.

I have in my possession a bound volume of the *Eastern Counties Magazine*, edited by the Hon. Mary Henniker, volume one of which covers August 1900 to May 1901. The pages are therefore extremely enlightening of the ending of the reign. Naturally enough, one page, heavily bordered by black, bears a poem, "In Memory, January 22, 1901". It begins:

> The century is dead,
>   Our Queen is gone;
> England with sinking head

And heart, droops on!
Shall our East Anglia stand
 Unmoved and dumb,
While from the sorrowing land
 Sad voices come?
Nay, all the fourscore years
 Her life has been
Tro' all our hopes and fears
 We loved our Queen.
No land o'er Earth's vast round
 Which owned her sway
A deeper note should sound
 Of pain to-day.
None held her rule more dear
 Than we who saw
Her every act revere
 God's Perfect Law.

Nay, though thy days have been,
 And thou art gone,
Good mother woman, Queen!
 Thy life goes on.

Not high poetry, perhaps, but expressive of the feelings of a great national bereavement of the time.

Although changes of an unprecedented character had taken place in the reign, the Suffolk countryside was much as it had been, certainly from mid-Victorian years. The towns had grown at the expense of the villages, but in the latter were the same old families, who spake the same old language. "Yow see hinder owd oaks, don't ye? But du, pra' cum in, for this dag (light rain or dew) is falling good tidy."

The villages were compact and there were no such things as council houses. The horse was still the chief means of locomotion and draught, with no signs or fears of a rival, so that the blacksmith and the wheelwright still flourished, with every village its smithy, and every village its builder's and wheelwright's yards, who would have been also the undertakers. In certain large villages one could find a carriage builder. Indeed, Suffolk was still an agricultural county, but not of the standard as flourished in the '50s and '60s.

However, the flash of the scythe was still seen in the harvest field; true, mechanical reapers were in use, but as the square of ripened corn grew smaller and smaller, so the rabbits attempted to escape, and the men and boys raced after them with sticks and shouts. The Lord of the harvest still ruled the day's labour, which was taken at a price; and in some cases largesse was still hollered and the gleaners gleaned. There was even a flail in my grandfather's shed.

Many of the old cottage homes still remained, full of bits and pieces that made one cottage like another. The long-cased clock in the corner, bearing a local name (in my grandfather's old home that of J. D. Bright of Saxmundham). The winged chair hiding a commode seat, the Suffolk chairs from a local market town, or, even from Mendlesham, the drop-sided table. Then upstairs the four-poster bed without which a bedroom was not furnished, the box at the foot draped in the same dimity as the bed valances. All these had come from earlier homes, including the bits of china, and the impedimenta on the backhouse mantelpiece. But paraffin lamps had ousted the rushlights, and matches the tinder-box. These were all in the natural order of things and had not yet been bought up by the antique dealers. This is no mere fancy writing, because my grandfather's home, and those of his many relations were the same from my personal remembrance.

Turning over the pages of the *Eastern Counties Magazine*, a good deal of space is given to two articles on "The Decline in our Rural Population", inspired by Rider Haggard's remarks on the subject at the Norfolk Chamber of Agriculture. The author states: "Some will ask, 'Has not the decline been greatly exaggerated?' I think not. In evidence I will ask the doubter to take what Cobbett would call 'a rural ride', and observe the numberless cottages to let, and also the vacant sites."

The rise in agricultural wages to 14s. a week, resulting in loss to the farmers is given as a cause. "Many farmers meet it in this way: they will pay, say, only £6 a week for labour, getting on very indifferently with eight men where hitherto they had employed half a score."

So the old lament had gone as voiced in the days of the lock-out. "Whoi yow know as well as I du, boys, if we was prize oxen, ship [sheep], or hosses, aye, even hogs, we should be better looked arter, better treated, aye an' thowt moor on tu."

A letter appeared as a result of the first article. "This has been felt more than ever before by farmers, inasmuch as many of them are considerably deficient in harvest-men. A farmer of more than fifty years standing writes that never before had he to commence harvest with a deficiency. Had the weather been opposite to the present, this would have been a very serious matter."

In his second article, the author gives the cause of the decline. First, the lower rate of wages prevailing in the country to that in town. Second, the railways and the penny post (above all things). He stated that very few rurals emigrate, though many migrate.

Thirdly, that the work for the skilled labour had removed to the towns. "The country shoemaker no longer makes shoes, but only mends. The village wheelwright is in a similar position, he has little to do but mend the wheels of the carriages, his employers buying the complete carriage from town makers. The blacksmith buys his horseshoes half made for him, while the brewers supply nineteen-twentieths of the beer drunk in the country, home brewed being nearly extinct. Country tailors have also become mere menders—the fact is, nearly all skilled work has left for the towns. I know no trade that has held its own so well as that of the harness maker." (He would have had a round-faced clock ticking on his wall, advertising Vanner and Prests' 'Molliscorium', which I believe was a kind of harness paste.)

As a cure the writer suggests a larger cultivation of barley, and the production of sugar beet, which might result "in a vast industry in this county, and bring back our land into cultivation".

A third article by another hand, deals with the question a little further. This instances the South African war and the great boom in trade and commerce, the development of the town improvements, making new railways, laying telephone wires, and the building mania everywhere. "Town life is more attractive, and the country, from its poverty and dearth of young folk, becomes more dull and monotonous." He further stated that the railways, the police force, and the town houses would attract the youths, and the more cheerful and better paid services in the cities would draw the maidens from the country.

The rural exodus affected the Country House also: "Of late years since the days of the agricultural depression, which really do exist, the number of servants in country houses in this part of England [Suffolk] has been much decreased. A butler, a footman, and perhaps six female servants, including the lady's maid, will now take the place of a former staff of at least a dozen."

It must be realized there were plenty of old people left in the villages who could recall the days of high farming. Their lament is well brought out in some verses subscribed by a James Blyth in dialect, under the title of *Tempus Actum*.

> They're a sluggin' an' widenin' miles o' the deaks (dykes)!
>> I reckon the whool mash 'ull sewn ha'e to goo!
> An' us ole mashmen 'ull fare like the freaks
>> I see last summer at Barnum's shoo!
> Fust come the railway, an' then come the bicycle:
>> Mowin' an' t'roshin machines an' all.
> Blaame! Theer ain't narthen to dew but to shy sickle
>> Flail an' winnower oover the wall.
>
> Paarson saay, 'Bill yew dew narthen but growl.'
>> Well bor! I reckon theer's plenty o' rayson!
> Wha'ss become o' the flightin' fowl?
>> I never see fifty the whool o' last sayson.
> Wha'ss become o' the gre't deeak eels? (dyke eels).
>> Shillin' a stoon we wuz glad to get for 'em.
> Gone! with the mallards an' snipe and teals!
>> If ye want any now yew ha' got to sweat for 'em.
>
> Wha'ss become o' the hoom-brewed bare?
>> (What they brew now is wuss 'an swanky)*
> Harvest suppers an' Christmas chare?
>> Never git narthen 'ats wuth a thanky.
> Wha'ss become o' the kind ole paarson?
>> He larnt us the Book, an' helped us i' trouble.
> This hare vicar dew narthen but fasten
>> Yar sins on yar back till they bend ye double.
>
> Wha'ss become o' the ole daame-schewl?
>> That larnt the young uns to reead an' write,
> To feear their God an' live by rule,
>> To labour by daay, an' sleeap at night.

* Swanky was a drink made by mashing malt a second time. It was in fact a second brew.

None o' yar rubbishin' schewl-booard taales,
   As the teeachers 'emselves doan't unnerstand,
Fillin' the wuckh'uses, cities, an' gaols;
   Draainin' the wark fro' the kind ole land.

Me an' the missus ha' seed enow on't,
   Blessin's to God the end is nigh.
Sewn we tew shall be maakin' our bow on't
   Never a tare an' never a sigh.
Each one 'ull goo to his own just plaace.
   One thing oonly I whooly trust—
I shan't lewse sight of har dare ole faace
   In the strange new life when our boons be dust.

However, as I can well remember, since I was 11 years old when the old Queen died, the country was still the country, something entirely different from that of today. Peaceful, soothing, lovely smelling, producing delectable food; and what sounds there were travelled a long distance. Think of the sky by day and the moonlit nights (the moonless ones terrified me), it provided a bliss unknown in a London street. And what of those cottage gardens, so delightfully kept, and so full of delicious perfume. They might have been as neat as a knot garden of old, or in a tangled profusion of stocks, wall-flowers, white pinks, mignonette, pansies and lavender; with bumble bees humming round in drowsy contentment.

But there was a fear amongst the old people that 'finis' might be written over the ways and methods of their inheritance. Expressed in my grandfather's oft repeated bit of wisdom: "The old uns can't, and the young uns 'ont!" Soon would see the end of the horses ambling homewards at the end of the day, jingling their harness and disturbing the dust as they made for the stables.

So the few intervening years passed, slowly and inevitably, to the first Great War. Something which men of enlightenment thought to be impossible, and the old life of the countryside came to an end.

The sun . . .
In dim eclipse disastrous twilight sheds
On half the nations, and with fear of change
Perplexes monarchs.
                                        Milton.

INDEX

⚜